THE AUGUSTAN REPRINT SOCIETY

JOHN BANKS   Y0-ATL-156

VERTUE BETRAY'D:

OR,

ANNA BULLEN

(1682)

Introduction by
DIANE DREHER

PUBLICATION NUMBERS *205 – 206*
WILLIAM ANDREWS CLARK MEMORIAL LIBRARY
UNIVERSITY OF CALIFORNIA, LOS ANGELES

1981

INTRODUCTION

Between 1677 and 1704 John Banks wrote seven tragedies and in 1706 he died. Little else is known about his life. He was educated for the law and later decided to try his hand at playwriting, first creating heroic plays and finally four tragedies based on Tudor history, thus helping to create a new genre known as the "she-tragedy"—that pathetic tragedy with a female protagonist later popularized by Nicholas Rowe.[2] Bank's last four plays, *The Unhappy Favourite*, *Vertue Betray'd*, *The Albion Queens*, and *The Innocent Usurper*, concern themselves with suffering innocence, thwarted love, court intrigues, treason, and beheadings. *Vertue Betray'd: Or, Anna Bullen*, a tragedy with a female figure as sole protagonist, is valuable for its historical, political, and dramatic significance.

The story of the enigmatic Anne Boleyn, second queen of Henry VIII, has long fascinated historians. Raised in the court of France to be spirited and flirtatious, Anne's deportment offered a striking contrast to pale Tudor standards of feminine behavior and beauty. Contemporary accounts described her lovely dark hair and flashing black eyes, but enemies criticized the dark coloring, the tall slender figure, the mole on her neck, and the irregular fingernail on one hand (which legend has extended to a sixth finger).[3] All agreed, however, that these charms were irresistible to the King, for Anne gave Henry VIII cause to renounce his religion and his first queen, the long-suffering Katherine of Aragon, thereby changing the course of English history. In her lifetime Anne was labeled a witch by her Catholic enemies and a martyr by the Protestants. Foxe's *Book of Martyrs* presents her as a Protestant saint, wronged by "some secret practising of the Papists" and vindicated by her heroic daughter Elizabeth.[4]

Banks portrayed Anne as a virtuous woman betrayed by the greed and ambition of those around her. Her honorable love for young Henry Percy, heir to the Earl of Northumberland, and their plans for marriage are thwarted by her ambitious father and brother, who conspire with Northumberland against the young couple, separating them and intercepting their letters, causing them unwittingly to break their vows in order to gratify the King's desires and their families' wish for advancement. The plight of innocent young lovers victimized by corruption and political intrigue was a favorite theme for Banks. In *The Innocent Usurper* Lady Jane Grey and Guilford Dudley are crossed by their parents' ambition. Other unfortunate couples are Mary and Norfolk in *The Albion Queens* and Essex and Rutland in *The Unhappy Favourite*. In each case, love is sacrificed to political ambition, providing a moment of passionate beauty all too soon cut off by the forces of darkness and all the more poignant for its brevity.

In *Vertue Betray'd* Banks has taken liberties with the chronology of history and made Cardinal Wolsey, who died in 1530, outlive himself, developing him as the consummate villain who plots with Elizabeth Blunt, the King's cast-off mistress, to destroy Anna. Banks has postponed Percy's marriage and condensed the actual events of 1533 to 1536 to fit within the space of five acts Anne's coronation, Katherine's death, Anne's execution, and Henry's courtship of Jane Seymour. Some difficulties with chronology understandably arise. As the play opens, "Anna" has apparently just married the King; in Act I "Piercy," who has been away from court, has not yet heard the news of the marriage that stunned England and all of Europe. By Act V, however, the young Princess Elizabeth is old enough to argue theology with her father and plead for her mother's life. Even the legendary precocity of the child Elizabeth, who was able when two years old to walk and talk like a child of four,[5] could not justify such compression. In spite of his obvious disregard for the unity of time, Banks has nevertheless given us a moving play. Its intricate plot with one emotional scene following closely upon another arouses considerable pity and fear.

The principal source for this play was *The Secret Novels of Queen Elizabeth*, an anonymous French romance translated into English in 1680, just two years before the first performance of *Vertue Betray'd*.[6] Several parallels can be found between these two accounts of the Anne Boleyn story, including the parents' conspiracy to separate Anna and Piercy and the love letters from Rochford to Blunt, later used to condemn Anna.

The popularity of plays about Anne's magnificent daughter undoubtedly stimulated Bank's imagination. Shakespeare and Fletcher's *Henry VIII* (1613), which ends with Cranmer's prophetic vision of Elizabeth's reign as Gloriana, was revived twice during the Restoration, once in 1663 and again in 1672.[7] In 1667 Thomas Heywood's *Queen Elizabeth's Troubles, and the History of Eighty*

Eight was produced,[8] and in 1680 an anonymous play, *The Coronation of Queen Elizabeth: With the Restoration of the Protestant Religion; or, The Downfal of the Pope* was performed at Bartholomew and Southwark Fairs. In 1681 Banks's *The Unhappy Favourite; or, The Earl of Essex* was presented by the King's company.[9] But the Restoration Theatre was not merely fascinated by the drama of the virgin queen's life and person; during the seventeenth century Queen Elizabeth acquired a symbolic value as the representative of truth, duty, and patriotism and the champion of the Protestant cause. It is apparent that Banks himself regarded her as such. His "Prologue Intended to be Spoken" to *The Unhappy Favourite* proclaims of Elizabeth:

> So her great Father was the first that struck
> Rome's *Triple Crown; but she threw off the Yoak:*
> *Straight at her Birth new Light the Heav'ns adorn'd,*
> *Which more than Fifteen hundred years had mourn'd.*[10]

In Anna's prophetic speech at the end of *Vertue Betray'd*, she sees her young daughter Elizabeth overcoming the Pope and vindicating her mother's reputation:

> That holy Tyrant,
> Who binds all *Europe* with the Yoak of Conscience,
> Holding his Feet upon the Necks of Kings;
> Thou shalt destroy, and quite unloose his Bonds,
> And lay the Monster trembling at thy Feet.
> When this shall come to pass, the World shall see
> Thy Mothers Innocence reviv'd in thee.
>
> (p. 74)

Although Banks protested in his prologue that *Vertue Betray'd* "meddles not with either Whig, or Tory" (sig. A4), the play contains a number of veiled contemporary political allusions. It was produced in the wake of the Popish Plot, a turbulent atmosphere in which scarcely a tragedy or comedy was written without some political allusion. The claims in 1678 of Titus Oates and Israel Tongue to have uncovered a Jesuit plot to murder the King and restore Roman Catholicism to England provoked a wave of hysteria and suspicion that precipitated a series of trials, further disclosures, exclusion bills, and active resentment of James, Duke of York, the Catholic heir to the throne. The annual Pope-burning pageants on 17 November were mobbed, and there was so much

direct interest in the "drama" of the Plot itself that theatre atten-
dance declined markedly,[11] a fact Dryden lamented in his epilogue
to *The Unhappy Favourite* in 1681. As politics became more
dramatic, the drama became more political, sometimes even
unexpectedly. In February of 1680 during a performance of John
Crowne's *The Misery of Civil-War* "some Gentlemen in their
Cupps" entered the Duke's Playhouse, threw candles and links at
the actors, cursed the Duke of York and several of his faction, and
concluded with a resounding cheer to the Protestant Duke of
Monmouth.[12] In 1679 the direct Protestant offensive began in the
theatres with a series of plays which either ridiculed or denounced
Catholicism, among them: Lee's *Caesar Borgia*, 1679; *The History
of Pope Joan*, an anonymous play privately presented in 1679;
followed by Settle's *The Female Prelate: Being the History of the
Life and Death of Pope Joan* in 1680; the anonymous *Coronation
of Queen Elizabeth; With the Restauration of the Protestant Religion; Or the Downfall of the Pope*, 1680; "the Plotting Papists
Litany," performed for the Lord Mayor's Show in London in
1680; Dryden's *The Spanish Fryar*, 1680; Shadwell's *The Lancashire
Witches, And Tegue O'Divelly the Irish Priest*, 1681; and an
anonymous farce, *Rome's Follies, or The Amorous Fryars*, presented
privately in 1681.

As examples of political allegorizing during this period *The
Coronation of Queen Elizabeth* deals with the discovery of a papist
plot to murder the Queen and Settle's *Female Prelate* offers a
harsh criticism of any monarch who would submit himself to the
Pope:

> By Heavens he's both a Coward and a Slave.
> *Romes* upstart Idol 'bove his Throne he rears,
> And servilely creates the God he fears,
> Down goes his Majesty, and down his Fame,
> Pope is the King, and Monarch but the name.[13]

Similar allegorical examples appear in *Vertue Betray'd*. Banks's
anachronistic representation of Wolsey cannot be attributed to a
historical oversight; Cavendish's *Life of Wolsey* made the story
too familar for that. By combining the villainy of Wolsey with
that of Thomas Cromwell and further emphasizing his degeneracy
by giving him a liaison with Blunt and proud ranting speeches
in which he boasts of his ability to manipulate the King, Banks
made the Cardinal an evil caricature of the Catholic Church
·-elf. Blunt's speeches associate the Cardinal with Alexander VI,

the notorious Borgia Pope, intensifying the villainous caricature yet more.

Beneath the piteous tale of thwarted love in this play, a political morality emerges. Blunt despises Anna because she is her rival, but Wolsey hates Anna because her religion threatens his political power: "A *Lutheran* Queen upon the Throne of England" (p. 3). The factions, then, are polarized by religion: Anna, the wronged innocent, becomes a Protestant martyr and her daughter, Elizabeth, even in her youth a champion of the Protestant cause, sees through Wolsey's elaborate equivocations, recognizing him as a diabolical "Picture of the Pope" (p. 67). Blinded by his lust, Henry cannot see Wolsey's villainy until the end of the play, when he orders his revenge and vows to "break the Yoak" and rule alone, alluding to the dangers that occur when Kings are dominated by the Papacy (p. 79). Banks's dedicatory epistle emphasizes his strong Protestantism as he praises the young Elizabeth, Duchess of Somerset, and her new husband for their allegiance to the Protestant cause: "*England* adores You for it . . . and the Chief of all, young *Edward*, its great Establisher, looks down with Joy to see his happy Successor lye in your Armes" (sig. A2v–A3).

That the play was revived on the stage and reprinted long after the Popish plot had passed attests to its dramatic as well as its political significance. First performed by the Duke's company in March of 1682,[14] it was well received, became a stock play, and was printed immediately. A revival and a second edition occurred in 1692, followed by another edition in 1705, more theater revivals, and twelve subsequent editions in the eighteenth century.

The play's dramatic antecedents include the tragedies of Beaumont and Fletcher and the heroic drama which directly preceded it. Beaumont and Fletcher were the most popular dramatists on the Restoration stage. Their elaborate plots, strong delineation of passions, tales of wronged love and suffering heroines fascinated Restoration audiences and exerted great influence upon the later drama. [15] All of these elements are present in *Vertue Betray'd*. The heroic drama, which Banks himself attempted some years before, is another important influence. Elizabeth Blunt, who rants, conspires, and seduces her way to power, is modeled after the lustful villainess of heroic tragedy. One aspect of heroic drama that figures largely in *Vertue Betray'd* is the dilemma of love and honor, in which the hero's duty to his king, country, and class, conflicts with his loyalty to his wife, friend, or lover.[16]

In the "she-tragedies" Banks transferred this conflict from the traditional male hero to the central female figure, who became the tragic protagonist in the play.[17] In *The Unhappy Favourite*, Elizabeth is torn between her duty as sovereign and her love for Essex—the personal and public worlds conflict. In *The Albion Queens* Elizabeth is similarly torn between her duty to her people and her affection for Mary Stuart. Lady Jane Grey in *The Innocent Usurper* accepts the crown only because her young husband threatens suicide, leading her to choose love over duty. Anna Bullen, of course, is caught in a moral dilemma between her duty as Henry's wife and her love for Piercy—two conflicting moral codes and two conflicting worlds. Banks's tragedies repeatedly focus on these two worlds in conflict and the sensitive and intelligent woman forced to deal with their irresistible and irreconcilable demands.

Anna's dilemma represents far more that the traditional opposition of courtly love to conventional mores. As Banks stresses repeatedly, Anna and Piercy were planning to be married; they had joined their hearts and honors in an exchange of vows or spousals, which at the least constituted a formal engagement, at most a legal marriage.[18] It is only their parents' ambition which violated this union, separating forever their public and private worlds. This is a fact which Piercy in his grief completely overlooks, persevering in his hopeless passion and longing for the fulfillment of a love which can no longer honorably exist. Whereas Piercy is overcome by self-pity, Anna is painfully aware of the dilemma which opposes these two allegiances, a conflict which wrenches her soul. She grieves that she has been false to her love against her will and realizes that now in her role as Henry's wife the situation is beyond her power to remedy. There is no solution in which she can affirm both love and honor. She at first avoids Piercy, realizing, as he does not, the duty her new status demands, a duty to her King, her country, to a world order in which a woman's prime virtues were obedience and chastity. Recognizing the dangers that any future encounters between them might bring, she agrees to see Piercy one last time, her love and pity debating with her duty in a series of asides. Much as she loves Piercy and realizes how much their families have wronged them, she remains true to her role as Henry's wife. Betrayed first by her family, then by Wolsey and Blunt, she returns love for hate and stoically meets her fate, suffering more for the pain of others—her brother, her child, the wronged Piercy—than for herself. In her final scenes she forgives Henry, embraces her brother, affirms her faith in God, and takes her leave of this world with grace and courage.

As a woman hero Anna is sensitive, intelligent, and clear-sighted, able to see through Wolsey's flattery, to recognize her fate, and to meet it with resolution. Limited in their scope to the domestic realm and courageous in their response to an unjust world rather than performing in the public world with the more active courage of traditional male heroes, Banks's women protagonists are heroes nonetheless. A number of reasons have been proposed to explain women's emergence as heroes in this period of English drama. Perhaps it was the presence of actresses upon the stage, perhaps a new and influential female audience; perhaps the change was related to the wave of feminism that swept through England in the late seventeenth century. The fact remains that Banks presented women as the heroes of these plays, not merely the heroines or female romantic leads but as the tragic protagonists who experience the inner conflicts and confront the moral dilemmas.

One might ask what values characterize a female tragic hero to distinguish her from her male counterparts. What is most arresting in all of Banks's women heroes is their ability to suffer courageously like their dramatic antecedents in Ford, Webster, Beaumont and Fletcher. If the tragic hero is defined primarily as the suffering victim of an unjust world, a view closer to melodrama than to classical tragedy, then in the seventeenth century, women, who presumably possessed a greater sensitivity than men with a corresponding lack of political power, began to be perceived in terms of their tragic potential. The redefinition of the hero that this new perception involved provides us with some important insights into the development of English drama. It indicates a new tragic sensibility emerging in the Restoration, in an England in which the optimism of an earlier age had been unsettled by the ravages of regicide and civil war. The humanism of the early Renaissance had emphasized competence, the individual's ability to improve his world through reason, and had given us in Shakespeare's tragedies heroes who precipitated their own fates by tragic choice or proairesis. But more and more this definition gave way in the Restoration to a bleaker view of the world in which the best one could do was to meet one's fate with courage and compassion. In this sense, Anna Bullen is a heroic figure, heroic beyond the measure of this mutable world.

University of Santa Clara
Santa Clara, California

NOTES TO THE INTRODUCTION

1. John Banks, *The Unhappy Favourite, Or The Earl of Essex*, ed. Thomas Marshall Howe Blair (New York: Columbia University Press, 1939), pp. 3–6.

2. Allardyce Nicoll, *A History of Restoration Drama 1660–1700* (Cambridge: Cambridge University Press, 1923), p. 156.

3. A. F. Pollard, *Henry VIII* (London: Goupil, 1902), 138–139; Hester W. Chapman, *Anne Boleyn* (London: Jonathan Cape, 1974), p. 128.

4. John Fox, *The Second Volume of the Ecclesiastical History: Containing the Acts and Monuments of Martyrs*, 9th edition. (London: 1684), II, 309.

5. Martin A. Sharp Hume, ed. *Chronicle History of King Henry VIII of England* (London: George Bell, 1889), p. 42.

6. Gerard Langbaine, *An Account of the English Dramatick Poets (1691)*, Intro. John Loftis (Los Angeles: William Andrews Clark Memorial Library, 1971), p. 8.

7. *The London Stage 1660–1800. Part I: 1660–1700*, ed. William Van Lennep (Carbondale: Southern Illinois University Press, 1963), pp. 72–74.

8. Van Lennep, p. 111.

9. Van Lennep, pp. 288, 295–96.

10. Blair, facsimile, p. [79].

11. George S. Whiting, "The Condition of the London Theatres, 1679–83: A Reflection of the Political Situation," *MP*, 25 (1927), 195–97; and "Political Satire in London Stage Plays, 1680–83," *MP*, 28 (1930), 34.

12. Van Lennep, p. 284.

13. Elkanah Settle, *The Female Prelate: Being The History of the Life and Death of Pope Joan. A Tragedy.* (London, 1680), I.ii.

14. Van Lennep, p. 308; Montague Summers in John Downes, *Roscius Anglicanus* (London: Fortune, 1928), reports that the play held the stage until 1766 (p. 226).

15. John Harold Wilson, *The Influence of Beaumont and Fletcher on Restoration Drama* (Columbus: Ohio State University Press, 1928); I am also grateful to Professor Nancy Cotton of Wake Forest University for sharing her ideas on the influence of Beaumont and Fletcher.

16. John E. Cunningham, *Restoration Drama* (London: Evans, 1966), p. 28.

17. Some critics have apparently overlooked this transferral of the heroic dilemma from the male to the female character. Eric Rothstein, for example, in *Restoration Tragedy* (Madison: University of Wisconsin Press, 1967) complains repeatedly of the weakness of Banks's male characters and their degeneration into "a new staple character for Restoration tragedy, the stupid hero . . . blatantly foolish or naive" (p. 96), but Rothstein fails to realize that the male characters he criticizes (Essex

in *The Unhappy Favourite*, Piercy in *Vertue Betray'd*, and Norfolk in *The Albion Queens)* are merely the male romantic leads, i.e., supporting actors, and that the heroes of these plays are women.

18. Lawrence Stone, *The Family, Sex and Marriage in England 1500–1800* (London: Weidenfeld and Nicolson, 1977), pp. 30–35.

BIBLIOGRAPHICAL NOTE

Vertue Betray'd (1682) is reproduced from a copy of the first edition in the William Andrews Clark Memorial Library (Shelf Mark: *PR3316/BZ1V5). A typical type-page (p. 11) measures 195 x 114 mm.

Vertue Betray'd:

OR,

ANNA BULLEN.

A

TRAGEDY.

ACTED at His

Royal Highness

THE

DUKE's Theatre.

Written by *JOHN BANKS*.

Crescit sub Pondere Virtus.

LONDON:

Printed for *R. Bentley* and *M. Magnes*, in *Russel-Street* in *Covent-Garden*. MDCLXXXII.

TO THE
ILLUSTRIOUS PRINCESS,
ELIZABETH,
DUTCHESS of
SOMERSET.

Madam,

Having met with Succefs in a Poem of this Nature, I was incourag'd to proceed, and lay the Scene again in a Country that, perhaps, hath not been, nor is now inferior for Heroick Perfonages to any part of the World; and if It is not fo efteem'd, it has been through the dulnefs of our Hiftorians, or the Ingratitude or Defigns of our Poets, who may think it an eafier Courfe to write of the Improbable and Romantick Actions of Princes remote, both by diftance of Time and Place, than to be confin'd at home, where ev'ry School-Boy has a right to be a Crittick, and ev'ry Gentleman an Intereft to ftand the Champion of his Family, againft a rafh and inconfiderate Author. I fay not this to derogate from thofe

excel-

The DEDICATION.

excellent Perfons, who, I ought to believe, have written more to pleafe their Audiences, than themfelves; but to perfwade them, as *Homer*, and our *Shakefpear* did, to Immortalize the Places where they were Born; and then, perhaps, I will fit down, and leave it to much abler Pens.

When I was refolv'd to do my Country this Juftice, where cou'd I pitch upon an *Hero* more confiderable, than out of Your Grace's Family? What Chronicle cou'd I confult, that would have inform'd me of a Greater? The very Crown it felf, oblig'd by fo many gallant Supporters, wou'd have told me a *Piercy*-----*Piercy* whofe Illuftrious Name and Blood, having for a long Series of years ran through the Perfons of fo many Earls of *Northumberland*: And if that ineftimable Chain was almoft broken, in the unfortunate Death of Your Father, it were never enough to be deplor'd, had not the Rich Treafure and Cryftal Stream of all your Predeceffors Blood and Vertues been ftor'd in You, which (now You have fubmitted to take a Noble Partner, as Angels have delighted to Converfe with Men) may prove the fecond and more lafting Fountain, from whence fhall fpring as many Princes more, and You reftore what the Great *Jocelin* had like to have loft. There is fo much of Divinity and Wifdom in Your Choice, that none but the Almighty ever did the like; and that was, when to the Solitary Firft of Men he gave a Wife, and with her, the World and *Eden* for a Dower: *England* adores You for it; the Proteftant Religion bleffes You; the Saints above
fing

The DEDICATION.

fing loud Your Praife, and the Chief of all, young *Edward*, its great Eftablifher, looks down with Joy to fee his happy Succeffor lye in your Armes. This great Day of *Jubile*, how doubly Fortunate has it made *Me*! fince this exalted Piece, which I defign'd for an humble Offering, may prove an *Epithalamium*! Long may You love, and live a thoufand Years, e're envious Death fhall part you; for every Day of fuch Illuftrious Lovers is more worth than whole Years of fordid Life befide. But why do I fuppofe that You fhould ever dye! You have a thoufand Charms, and Youth impregnable againft Deaths Batteries this many Ages yet; and who ever was fo happy as to fee your incomparable Mother, and how many Years of Beauty fhe has to come, will think that Yours fhall never fade, but always bloom: You look as if you had nothing Mortal in you; Your Guardian Angel fcarcely is more a Deity than You, and the bright Planet that fhin'd with fuch amazing Influence at Your Birth, makes not a more glorious Figure in the Heavens, than You on Earth.

When I made choice of fo excellent a Subject, I was not to feek for a Dedication: I was commanded to it, even by the good Fate of the Play: For before what Patronefs fhou'd I kneel, but Her, the Character of whofe great Anceftor was the chiefeft Stroak and Lineament that made it acceptable to the World? and it is as much Your Grace's due, as Firft-Fruits are to Monarchs. For *Anna Bullen*, though I drew her in all the nicaft *Ideas* that ever my Pen or Fancy could be capable of; yet, I confefs, fhe comes fhort of the

Ex-

The DEDICATION.

Excellency of Your real Perfections; and though her Merits rais'd her to a Crown, and she was Queen, her Fortunes were less Miraculous than Yours. For Heaven, without a Diadem, never showr'd down so many admirable Blessings of Virtue, Beauty, Birth, Wit, and Fortune, upon any One of Your Sex before. I dare no further attempt their Description with my Ignorance, lest I speak too Meanly or Irreverently of 'em; therefore I'le leave the mighty Subject to some more Glorious Pen: For none but a *Cowley*, or the best of *Laureats*, ought to write of you: My mean Stile has no other Ornament than Truth; and with that, and in all Humility, I return Thanks for Your most Gracious Acceptance of so poor a Trifle, which has scarce given a more happy Life to the Play, than it has to the Author, who is, Madam,

Your Grace's most Humble,

most Obedient, and

most Devoted Servant,

J. Banks.

PROLOGUE Spoken to *Anna Bullen*, written by a Person of Quality.

TO all *Impartial Judges in the Pit*,
    And ev'ry beauteous Patroness of Wit;
    I'm sent to plead the Poets Cause, and say,
    There's not one Slander in his modest Play.
He brings before your Eyes a modern Story,
Yet meddles not with either Whig, *or* Tory.
Was't not enough, vain Men of either side,
Two Roses once the Nation did divide?
But must it be in danger now agen,
Betwixt our Scarlet, *and* Green-Ribbon *Men?*
Who made this diff'rence, were not Englands *Friends*;
Be not their Tools to serve their Plotting Ends.
Damn the State-Fop, who here his Zeal discovers, }
And o're the Stage, like our ill Genius, hovers : }
Give us a Pit of Drunkards, and of Lovers ; }
Good Sanguine Men, who mind no State Affair,
But bid a base World of it self take Care:
We hope there lives not so abhorr'd a Thing,
But loves his Country, and wou'd serve his King.
But in your Parties, why should we engage, }
Or meddle with the Plots of a mad Age? }
We lose enough by those upon the Stage. }
Welcome Mask-Teazer, Peevish Gamster, Huffer ;
All Fools, but Politicians, we can suffer;
A Gods name, let each keep to his Vocation;
Our Trade is to mend You, *and not the Nation:*
Besides, our Author has this further End, }
'Tis not enough if but One Side's his Friend; }
He needs you All, his weakness to defend : }
And to oblige you to't, hopes he has shown
No Country has Men braver than your own.
His Hero's all to England *are confin'd*;
To your own Fathers (sure) you will be kind.
    He brings no Forreigners to move your Pity,
    But sends them to a Jury of the City.

The

PERSONS Reprefented.

KING Harry.	Mr. Smith.
Cardinal.	Mr. Gillow.
Northumberland.	Mr. Wiltfhire.
Piercy.	Mr. Betterton.
Rochford.	Mr. Jof. Williams.
Anna Bullen.	Mrs. Barry.
Lady Diana Talbot.	Mrs. Petty.
Lady Eliz. Blunt.	
Young Princefs Elizabeth.	

Ladies, Gentlemen, Attendants, and Guards.

SCENE

LONDON.

VERTUE

BETRAY'D:

OR,

Anna Bullen.

ACT I. SCENE I.

Enter Northumberland *and* Rochford.

North. THis is the Day fhall Crown your Parents wifhes,
And long expecting hopes: The King intends
To publifh ftreight hisMarriage with your Sifter,
And make her known by th' Title of his Queen:
The Reafon why it was fo long kept fecret,
Was our great Cardinal's Delays, and Tricks
Of *Rome*, which *Harry* has with Frowns difcover'd:
But fince, in fpite of *Woolfey* and the Conclave,
By Reverend *Cranmer* has the Caufe been try'd;
And *Katherine* is this day proclaim'd divorc'd.
   Roch. Heav'n be my Witnefs, brave *Northumberland!*
It joyes not me, but that it is his pleafure,
Whofe Happinefs we all are bound to pray for;
And may my Sifter's Crown fit lighter on
Her Brow, than does the Honour upon mine:
Something of boding whifpers to my Soul,
And tells me, Oh! this Marriage will be fatal——
Methinks I fee a Sword ty'd to a Thread,

B

Small

Small as a Hair, hang o're our Pageant Greatneſs:
Believe me, Friend ; Thrones are ſevereſt Touch-ſtones;
And, like the Emblem of their Guard, the Lyon,
All but of Royal-Blood they will deſtroy.

North. My Lord, this is ſevere to all that love you;
And you reflect unkindly on your Fortunes.

Roch. Fortune! why did ſhe lay her load on her ?
A load, I ſay, to quiet Minds——ſhe ſhould
Have caſt it upon one that was ambitious:
My Lord, it had been kindly done of Fortune,
T' have ſeen my Siſter wedded to her Vows,
Your *Peircy's* Wife ; and not at one time made her
Both Cruel to the Queen, and Falſe to him.

North. You know, my Lord, we all are Witneſſes
With what remorſe ſhe took the Regal Burthen,
That ſate upon her like a heavy Armour
On a Child's back ; ſhe ſtagger'd with the Weight.

Roch. Oh! may it not be fatal to us, Heav'n !
For at the very time ſhe gave her Hand
To th' eager King to faſten't with a Pledge,
The Ring fell off, and could no more be found.

North. Meer Chance, my Lord.

Roch. And then immediately,
When the glad Ceremonies were perform'd,
The amorous King bending to kiſs her Hand,
A ſhower of Pearls broke paſſage from her Eyes,
And all-bedew'd his Head with ominous Tears.

North. The common uſe of every baſhful Bride.

Roch. What will ſhe do when ſhe ſhall underſtand
Our foul Deſigns, and *Peircy's* Innocence ;
His Letters to her that you intercepted,
And counterfeited others to deceive her,
To make her once believe that he was marry'd ?
But what a mortal Grief will ſeize your Son,
When he ſhall find his Miſtreſs was betray'd ;
And forc'd to marry one ſhe cannot love ?

North. To prevent that : Soon as he's come to Court,
Juſt but to ſee ſhe's marry'd, and no more,
(Not giving him the time for ſecond thoughts)
I'll make a Match between him and the Heireſs

Of

Of *Shrewsbury*.
   Roch. A very gallant Lady.
As Virtuous, Beautiful, and Richer far
Than all our Generation of that Sex.
   North. You wrong your self to flatter me. Her Father
Brings her this day on purpose from the Country:
But the Queen thinks already they are marry'd.
   Roch. And are you sure to gain your Sons consent,
To what he has been still so obstinate?
   North. Rage and Despair, when he shall find her false,
Will make him rashly change to any state;
And, thinking to be miserable, will plunge
Into the dreadful Sea of Matrimony,
And make himself, though much against his Will,
The happiest man that ever was on Earth.

Enter Cardinal Woolsey *musing.*

Behold the proud imperious Cardinal,
With such a furious Tempest on his Brow,
As if the World's four Winds were pent within
His blustering Carkass. He has heard the News,
And comes to argue with his Friend the Devil,
The Reason of his No-Intelligence
   Roch. The Popedom now, and all the Wealth in *Rome,*
Can scarcely recompence him for the fright
This News has put him in———See how he staggers,
Giddy with th' height his Pride has rais'd him to.
'Tis then most fatal to unhappy *England*
When such Church Blazing-Stars appear in it.[*Ex.* North. *and* Roch.
   Card. Marry'd in private, and declar'd his Queen!
Katherine divorc'd, and *Anna Bullen* marry'd!
Now, by our Holy Father's Triple-Crown
It must not, cannot, nay, it shall not be.
Where was your aid, that time, you slothful Saints,
You whom false Zeal created in more numbers
Than e're the Heathen made and worshipp'd Gods?
A *Lutheran* Queen upon the Throne of *England*!
She to lye in the Bosom of our Prince!
A Buxom King, that for a wanton Smile
Will pawn his Faith, and turn an Heretick!
       Enter

Enter the Lady Elizabeth Blunt.

Blunt. Awake thou wretched dreaming Prieft, look up:
Can you behold your proud Saint *Peter* fhake?
The mighty Pillar of that fpreading Church
That holds the great Religion of the World
To ftagger, and beftow no help, no aid
From mighty *Woolfey*'s Shoulders to fupport it?
Is this the great King-Cardinal, who late
From fmalleft Root began to fhade the Land,
And ftood the talleft Cedar of the Church?
Shame to thy Prieft-hood, and thy Scarlet Robe,
Ev'n thou to whom the liberal See of *Rome*
Has given all, next giving of her felf:
Unworthy Servant of fo kind a Miftrefs.
  Card. What does the Faireft mean!
  Blunt. Ha! muft I teach thee?
Art thou the Thing that from the Chaff of Mankind,
From the bafe fcurrilous Rubbifh of the World,
Firft found thy felf a way to thrive by Wit?
Then edging it with fharpeft Villanies,
Mow'd thee a paffage to thy Princes Breaft,
And cut down all the Virtuous from his fight,
Who chofe thee for the Champion of his Vices;
Whilft thou with labour let loofe all their Sluces,
And pour'd them like a Torrent in his Bofom?
This you did once confefs to me, and more,
When you declar'd how hot you were in love——
Bullen is Queen, the Crown you promis'd me
Now wreaths her Head——Are thefe the hopes you gave me,
When once you faid my Son fhould be a King?
The News not ftirs your Wonder! Hell and Furies!
  Card. What wou'd you I fhould do to ferve you?
  Blunt. Forgive me, tender *Woolfey*, pious Cardinal!
Shall I then teach your Scarlet Priefthood Blood?
I would have done as *Alexander* did,
The Sixth, and the moft merciful fo nam'd;
Are there no Confecrated Weapons left?
Or have you loft the Power to make 'em fo?

Give

Give me Saint *Dagger* or Saint *Poison* ſtraight,
And I will do that Meritorious Act:
Diſpatch her ſtreight to Hell, from whence ſhe fetch'd
Thoſe Looks that robb'd me of the King and Crown.
 Card. Have patience, Madam.
 Blunt. Preach it to the Damn'd,
To thoſe that feel the Rack or Inquiſition——
Curſe on your Gown Apologies: but more
Be curſt the time of *Bullen's* fatal Birth,
Wrinkles like Age anticipate her Youth;
Mildews and Blaſts devour her wanton Beauties,
Small-Pox and Leproſies rough-caſt her o're;
Dig up her Charms and Features by the Roots,
And bury 'em in Pits as deep as Graves.
 Card. Study ſome Act that may revenge this Fury,
This hurts no more than Barks of Coward Curs;
She lives, and is as beautiful as ever:
Be rul'd by me, who like a dreadful Piece,
Am ſure to kill, where-e're I take my aim,
Before they hear the Noiſe or ſee the Flame.
 Blunt. Oh tell me how to quench this Fire within!
That burns me up with thoughtful Injury.
 Card. An eaſie way I'le chalk to your Revenge,
A Road not ſteep, nor dangerous, but ſmooth;
So unſuſpected, and ſo fatal too,
That the Queens Fancy and deluded Genius,
Shall tempt her in the ſame diſſembled Path,
Taking her by the other hand with us,
And lead her in the Pit prepar'd for her.
 Blunt. Go on my *Woolſey*, charming as the young,
And more melodious than a Quire of Angels.
 Card. This then it is: The King you know's inconſtant,
As jealous and as teaſty as old Age,
So covetous of the pleaſure he poſſeſſes,
That he who does but look upon't muſt dye,
With her, whoſe innocent Charms did force him to't.
 Blunt. But how ſhall we be backt with a pretence?
 Card. 'Tis eaſie to give fire to that fond Breaſt
That is already charg'd with jealous Sulphur:
The Queen loves *Piercy*, that may be a means;

And Spies may be laid every where to watch
Their Private Meetings, and their very looks,
And then acquaint the Hot-brain'd King with it:
So ſtreight their joyful Deſtinies are ſeal'd.
    Blunt. Moſt admirable!
    Card. If we fail in this,
Some cry'd-up Beauty, ne're yet ſeen at Court,
Muſt be found out, to put her in his way,
And take the Amorous King: 'Twill certain do;
For then no greedy Falcon, when he ſees the Lure,
Will flye down ſwifter to be catch'd and hooded,
Than he into the Fetters of her Charms.
    Blunt. O come to my Embrace, thou Godlike Prieſt!
Balm to my wounded and my tortur'd Boſom.
    Card. Go ſtreight, and haſte about the Intelligence.
    Blunt. I will. Good Fortune has been ſo propitious,
To make young *Rochford,* *Anna Bullen's* Brother,
Enamour'd of my Beauty; him I'le mould,
Sound ev'ry thought of his unguarded Soul,
Linking him cloſe in amorous Intrigues,
'Till I have diſcover'd from him our Deſign
Of *Peircy's* Love, and of his Siſters Conduct.
    Card. An Accident, the luckieſt that could happen!
Behold the Queen in her firſt State and Greatneſs,——
But yet ſhe bears it with no welcome meen:
Peircy hangs heavy on her heart, and in her Eyes;
It works, it manages as we would have it:
And in her heedleſs Innocence ſhe fails,
Shunning no Rocks, no Quick-ſands, nor no Danger,
But runs into her Ruine faſter than
We wiſh.
    Blunt. Her Crown is hideous to my ſight,
Its Jewels fatal as the Eyes of Baſilisks:
O Cardinal! This Rival-Queen and I
Should never meet but in the Scales of Death,
That weigh all Mortals even and alike.

Queen Anne *appears seated upon a Throne.* Northumberland, Rochford, *Lords, Ladies, Attendants and Guards about her.*

Omnes. Long live King *Henry*, and Queen *Anne* of *England*.
North. Immortal live Great Queen of *England*, *France*,
And *Ireland*, and for ever rule the Heart
Of Conquering *Henry*, as he Reigns o're us
And all his faithful Subjects———
I speak it as the Wishes and the Voice
Of your most Loyal Kingdoms; to confirm it,
Sound straight your loudest Instruments of Joy,
And shout as I do, all that love their Queen.
    Queen rises from her Throne, [*Shouts and Trumpets within.*
Queen. These Sounds might lift another to the Heav'ns!
But what is Musick to the Ear that's deaf;
Or Crowns and Scepters to a dying Wretch ?
Despair turns all alike that comes to me,
Blind to the Pomp that glads all Eyes but mine,
Deaf to its Charms, and dead to all its Glories.
       [*Trumpets and Shouts again.*
Cease you more empty Flatterers than Winds;
Be silent as the Sorrows in my Breast :
If you will give me ease, forbear such Flatteries:
For I receive 'em with as little joy,
As ev'n those silly Wretches utter them,
Having no other Reason but vile Custom.
My Noble Lords!
I know you all are Loyal to the King,
And for his sake you are thus kind to me ;
But for the Rabble, who can read that *Sphinx* ?
Their very Breath that now Proclaims, with joy,
Sad *Katherine* to be no longer Queen,
And my unwelcome Coronation,
Would the same moment, should my Stars permit,
Shout louder at the Sentence of my Death.
 Card. Most glorious and beloved of *England*'s Queens
O lay not on our Nation such a Curse,
As a suspicion of its Faith to you.
I dare be bold, and say it, as a Priest,

As Confeſſour to all my Country's Guilt,
There's none, how mean ſoever with my ſelf,
But loves you more than life, or darling Riches,
Wiſhing to feel ſevereſt Penance here,
And Hell hereafter, rather than behold
You leſs a Queen, or leſs ador'd than now.

Queen. They have my thanks, next kind good natur'd *Woolſey,*
Who cannot but be real, 'cauſe he ſays it.

Card. Oh that your Majeſty would think ſo ever,
And that my proud endeavours, with ſuccefs,
Firſt whiſper'd in the Boſom of the King
The ſecret Wonders of your Mind and Perſon,
And made him ſoon diſcover all your Beauties,
Thoſe rare Perfections, that above your Sex
Have merited his Paſſion and his Crown.

Queen. O Reverend, pious, beſt of Cardinals!
Who too well knows
By whoſe high hand I climb'd this malic'd Greatnefs,
And wear this envy'd Crown.

Card. May Heav'n and Stars
Pour their juſt hatred on——

Queen. Ceaſe Execrations;
For ſhould they come to paſs, as Heav'n forbid,
What wou'd the miſerable Nation do?
Beſides 'twere pity to the King and me,
That we ſhould loſe ſo exquiſite a Head,
And ſuch a Prelate ſhould be damn'd ſo ſoon

Card. Ten thouſand Saints, more than my Royal Maſter,
Are Witneſſes to th' truth of what I ſay.

Queen. As many Saints and Myriads of bright Angels
Can witneſs of the blackneſs of thy Soul,
That canker'd firſt the Conſcience of thy Maſter,
Miſleading him with hopes to purge a ſin,
To act the worſt, ev'n a Religious Guilt——

Card. The wiſe and juſt Omnipotence ——

Queen. No more:
Hell's not ſo full of Torments, as thy Soul
Has Blaſphemies to be rewarded in it——
Give me ſome eaſe, juſt Heav'n! if there be any——
My Lords! if there's no more for you to act

To

To perfect or unmake this Ceremony,
(Oh that it cou'd be done!) retire a while,
And leave me with my Women for some Moments———
What am I then a Prisoner to be guarded?
Has then a Throne cost me so dear a Price,
As forfeit of my Liberty of Thinking?
Do Princes barter for their Crowns their Freedoms?
Good Heav'n! not think! nor pray if I have need———
If I am Queen, why am I not obey'd?
 Card. We'll all perform your Majesties Command.
         [*Ex. all but her Women.*
 Queen. Am I got loose, loose from this worrying Scene
Of dismal State, that always loads a Monarch,
And racks him with dissembling Torturers?
O wretched state of Princes! that want nothing
But a Retreat from Business and from Crowds;
Yet wanting that, want every thing that's happy,
A Soul at ease———O sacred Solitude!
How aiery and delightful are thy Walks?
No stinging Serpent, nor worse Insect Man,
Disturb thy fragrant and enamell'd Paths;
No Winter-Blasts, nor *Autumn* Winds molest
Thy sacred Grotto's, all around is Summer;
Nothing broods there but an Eternal Spring,
Mild as all *May*, and Beautiful as *Eden* :
Thou charitable Good! that from th' afflicted
Unloads the heavy Burdens that oppress them,
And plants Repose in every Breast in stead!

Enter a Lady.

 Lady. The Lady *Diana Talbot* begs admittance,
To pay her Duty to your Majesty.
 Queen. What say'st! Thou'st rous'd a Dragon in my Breast,
Which I had thought for ever to have husht:
That Name sets every Pulse again at work
Within me———*Talbot !* how art thou mistaken?
She's *Piercy's* now ; And *Piercy* all his hers.
 Lady. Shall she be brought to your Presence?
 Queen. Ay—No—Yes———

Do any thing, fo 'twill be fure to kill me:
O *Piercy! Piercy!* would thou ne're hadft been
Unfaithful, or at leaft in being fo,
Hadft never taught me how to be reveng'd:
But oh the difmal Pain is all my own,
And like an Arrow from an o'rebent Bow,
The hafty Dart turn'd back and hurt my felf,
Wounding that Breaft where I leaft meant my aim.
How foft and tender were our mutual Vows,
Which fince another's Charms, like Lightning, blafted;
Whilft Parents Threats and Kings Authority,
Rent me, like Thunder, from my fixt Refolves:
Th' art marry'd now, and all thofe amorous fighs,
And paffionate tears, with thoufand Extafies,
Which we both learnt and taught to one another,
Like innocent Children in the School of love,
Are now the Arts with which, falfe man! th' haft caught
Anothers fond believing heart, they are.

Enter Lady Diana Talbot.

She comes, triumphant in her Eyes the joy
That once like Tides o're-flow'd my fruitful Breaft.
How proud fhe bears her felf to fee my pain!
Whilft I look up to her, and figh in vain!
But I will hide it, and forgive me Heav'n;   [Diana *kneels.*
For 'tis the firft time that I e're diffembled———
" Rife dear *Diana,* you have been a Stranger;
Could nothing but a Queen drag you to Court;
I owe this Kindnefs to my Royalty,
And not your Friendfhip———
     Dian. Pardon, mighty Princefs!
I had been bleft for ever in your Prefence,
Charming in all Eftates as well as now,
Had I been Miftrefs of my Inclinations.
But———
     Queen. 'Tis no matter, I'le allow your Reafon,
A Caufe fo indifpenfible and juft,
That 'twere a fault in me to blame fuch Virtue
     Dian. Indeed a Parents Will ought ftill to be

                                        Obey'd,

Obey'd, next Duty to your Majefty.

Queen. And fomething yet more binding—Do not blufh—
Come I'le unriddle all, and fpare your Tongue
The trouble, and your bafhful Cheeks the Fire.

Dian. What fire ? what blufhes do you tax me with?
I feel not any but what Wonder raifes,
And blufh becaufe I cannot comprehend.

Queen. You are unkind, why make it you a fecret?
And but to me, when all the World reports it.

Dian. There is no fecret; nothing I would hide
From fo ador'd a Friendfhip as my Queen's.

Queen. Why d' you fufpect me then? [*Afide*] How loth fhe is
To tell it me! As loth as I to hear it:
Sure fhe fufpects how fatal 'twill be to me;
And the proud man has triumph'd o're my weaknefs!
And told her all my paffion with a fcorn——
'Tis fo; whilft poor, regardlefs, innocent I
Was all the while their Cenfure and their Paftime,
The Fool, whofe Story acted made 'em fport,
And gave new edge to all their fated Joyes;
Nay and perhaps drew Pity from their Pride?
Pity! good Gods! muft I endure their Pity?
You will not own it then? But 'tis no matter.   [*To* Diana.
When faw you *Piercy* ?

Dian. Piercy, Madam!   [*She ftarts.*

Queen. Yes,
Why did you ftart! has he a Name fo horrid?
But now you fpoke as tho there were not fuch
A man i'th' World, and wonder'd at my meaning;
But yet have all the Agonies to hear him nam'd:
Him you would hide, but cannot hide your Blufhes.

Dian. Good Heav'n! by what ftrange Miracle have you [*afide.*
Reveal'd my fecret Paffion to the Queen?
I never told my Grievance but to you,
And that but filently in broken Sighs
And ftifled Tears——

Queen. 'Tis plain fhe is difturb'd!——
What can this mean? Sure one of us is mad!   [*Afide.*
Why all this Care to hide a Truth from me,
That is the common talk of all the World?

There's

There's fomething in it more than yet I know,
Which I muft fearch into by other means.
Madam, I thought when I had condefcended   [*To* **Diana.**
To open my Breaft, and mingle Friendfhips with you,
You would not then deny fo fmall a Secret ;
And now when I am Queen and may command it———
Therefore begone. Leave me without Reply.
Henceforth I'le know the Perfons better, out
Of whom I mean to chufe a Friend———Farewell———
Piercy no doubt is not fo fondly nice,
But brags, and tells the World of his proud Conqueft.

   Dian. Forgive me firft ; then give me leave to tell you———
How 'twas difclos'd to you, the Wonder ftuns me ;
But *Piercy* knows not yet, nor fhall from me,
This fecret which I thought fcarce Heav'n found out.

   Queen. Racks and worfe Tortures! Frenzies of the mind!
Hence ; take her from my fight : fhe will diftract me.

   Dian. O hear me firft : your Fury's not fo dreadful,
As is my pain to tell : yet I'le confefs :   [*Kneels.*
A fatal Truth it is, *Piercy* I love———
Now pity me, and quench my torturing Blufhes :
For Heav'n reveal'd it to you for no Ill.

   Queen. I am amaz'd : ftill worfe and worfe, fhe ftabs me,
And they're Abufes all———Ingrateful Woman!
Wouldft have me think thy lawful Paffion fuch a wonder!
Is it a Crime for thee to love thy Husband ?

   Dian. Ha! what is that you fay ? my Husband faid you!
Meant you to mock th'unfortunate *Diana* ?

   Queen. No. I will fay't again ; thy perjur'd Husband!

   Dian. Ah! Royal Madam! *Piercy* is more bleft ;
We are not Marry'd, he is not my Husband.

   Queen. Ha!   [*Afide.*

   Dian. That were to me too great a Happinefs!

   Queen. Should this be true, what will become of me ? [*Afide.*
Diana rife : Are you not Marry'd, faid you !

   Dian. So far from that, his Perfon I've not feen
In twelve long Months, this laft long tedious year.

   Queen. Art not his Wife!

   Dian. By all your precious Hopes
And mine, I'm not.

                                Queen.

Queen. Is *Piercy* then not marry'd!
Support me Heaven ! and with a wonder fave me;   [*Afide.*
Call all thy Virtue and thy Courage ftreight
To help thee now, or thou art loft for ever.
Am I then cheated! and is *Piercy* faithful !
If I can bear all this, I challenge *Atlas*
To live under a Load fo vaft as mine.
Ah *Piercy*! injur'd *Piercy*! injur'd *Bullen !*
But hold, there's yet a greater task behind,
And that is to Diffemble well.————*Diana* !

    Dian. Madam————

    Queen. Thou wonder'ft at my Curiofity,
As tho I were concern'd at this falfe Story.
I'll tell thee why: It has been long reported,
That you and *Peircy* were in private Marry'd.

    Dian. Such a report came likewife to my hearing;
But how 'twas rais'd, by whom, or why, I know not.

    Queen. Too well the dreadful caufe of it I know.   [*Afide.*
This, when I heard, I took unkindly from you:
I was your Friend, you ought no more to fteal
A Marriage from a Friend, than from a Father.
And when you aggravated, as I thought,
By your unkind denial, it enrag'd me;
For which I hope, *Diana*, you'll forgive me————
Methinks I do it rarely————   [*Afide.*

    Dian. Beft of **Queens**!
Thus on my Knees, I ought to beg that pardon:
I only did offend, my Gracious Miftrefs.

    Queen. Rife to my Arms————This Kifs now Seals thee mine
For ever.

    Diana. Oh moft admirable Goodnefs !

    Queen. This tendernefs betrays me, melts my Soul !   [*Afide.*
A fatal Engine that draws all my Griefs
Up to my Eyes and Lips, juft ready to unload
And pour 'em in at once into her Breaft,
Whom I, of all the World, fhould hide 'em from.
Oh for fome Wild, fome Defart to complain in,
Some vaft and uninhabitable place;
Or elfe fome Precipice that butts the Ocean,
The wide, and never to be fathom'd Ocean,

That

That I might tell the ecchoing Rocks my Woes,
And count my Sorrows to the Winds and Seas,
More pitiful, and more relenting far,
Than falſe and cruel Mankind is to me.

Dian. You ſeem diſturb'd ! Ah*!* what inhumane Grief
Dares ſeize your Royal Breaſt ?

Queen. Come, dear *Diana*;
Go to my Cloſet with me ; there, perhaps,
Some reſt may quell this melancholly Monſter;
And there it may not be amiſs ſometimes
To talk of *Peircy*, will it ?

Dian. Sacred Queen,
'Twill not ; and oh ! I wiſh that the Diſcourſe
Would ſooth your Soul with as much Joy as mine.

Queen. Theſe are the firſt of Miſeries, the reſt
Come rolling on apace, and, *Katherine*, now
Thou art Reveng'd——Juſt Heav'n, whoſe is the Sin ?
Puniſh not me, I ſought not to be Queen ;
But *Henry*'s Guilt amidſt my Pomp is weigh'd,
And makes my Crown ſit heavy on my Head,
To baniſh from his Bed, the chaſteſt Bride,
That twenty years lay loving by his ſide !
How can I give it, without Tears, a Name,
When I reflect my Caſe may be the ſame ?
And I, perhaps, as Slaves are by the Prieſt,
Thus gay and fine for Sacrifice am dreſt.
Ah ! *Katherine*, do not envy me thy Throne,
For thou art far more happy that has none.   [*Exeunt.*

The End of the Firſt Act.

ACT.

ACT II. SCENE I.

Enter Northumberland and Rochford.

Rock. THE News is ſtrange you tell me of the King.
    North. Moſt wonderful, nor can I gueſs the meaning,
He came juſt now from Hunting as his uſe,
Where at Sir *Thomas Seymour*'s Houſe he was
Moſt ſplendidly and kindly entertain'd
At a Repaſt.
    Roch. Took he there any thing
Amiſs?
    North. No: quite contrary, ſo good humour'd,
I never ſaw him in my life more pleaſant:
But now, inſtead of going to the Queen,
With words that ſhew'd more diſcontent than rage,
He order'd all about him to retire,
And, which is ſtill more ſtrange, enquir'd for *Woolſey*,
Woolſey, whom all men thought quite out of favour;
Then ſhut himſelf within his Bed-Chamber,
And there remains; nor durſt the boldeſt venture
To follow him, and ask him what he ails——
May not the Queen your Siſter, think you, be
The innocent Occaſion?
    Roch. That's impoſſible!
For but laſt Night he came to her Apartment,
With all the heat and love that could inſpire
A Bridegroom, ſcarcely of an Hour's making:
With haſte he ran, and where he ſhould have ſate
He kneel'd down by her as his Deity;
Printing ſoft Kiſſes on her lovely Hand,
And ſigh'd as if he had been ſtill a Woeing.
    North. Right *Harry* ſtill: for by this Flood of Paſſion
The nearer he's to Ebb and Change.
    Roch. See! the King.
    North. You are Brother to his Wife, and may be bold,
But I'le not venture.   [*Ex.* North.
                                        Enter

Enter King Harry.

King. Who are you that durft prefs on my Retirement?
Ha! *Bullen!* Get thee from my fight—Begone—— [*Ex.*Roch.
Who waits there? Why am I thus troubled?
Let none but *Woolfey* dare to be admitted.   [*To the Attendants.*
Who can withftand fo vaft a fhock of Beauties,
So many Wonders in fo bright a Form?
When Heav'n defigns to make a perfect Face,
A Beauty for a Monarch to enjoy,
'Tis feign'd that the moft skilful Spirits are all
Imploy'd, and juft before their Eyes is plac'd
Th' exacteft, lovelieft Angel for a Pattern;
If it be true; this only muft be fhe,
And muft be mine——Who's there? the Cardinal?

Enter Woolfey.

Card. The humbleft Vaffal of his God-like Mafter.
King. Come hither, Sir——I fent for thee, my *Woolfey!*
And doft not wonder; when but yefterday
I took from thee the Seal and Chancellour's Place?
But 'tis no matter: Do not care, I fay:
I love you ftill in fpight of all your Foes——
You have malicious Enemies at Court;
Befides the Queen, my Lord, is no good Friend
Of yours.
Card. Wretched am I that have incurr'd
My Kings Difpleafure, and my Queens dire Hatred!
But m' Innocence when I am dead, perhaps
May to my Royal Mafter, tho too late
Appear.
King. Talk not of Death, good Cardinal,
For I have Bufinefs with thee firft——By Heav'n!
He that dares mutter *Woolfey* is a Traitor,
Shall dye for a worfe Traitor as he is:
Keep thy own ftill, the Bifhopricks of *York*
And *Winchefter*, and Cardinal, that is
Above my Grant; and when I give thee leave,

Go

Go to thy Diocefs, and live to fpite 'em.

Card. Immortal Wreathes, and Diadems of Saints,
Crown you in Heav'n for this Royal Goodnefs.
I am grown old, too weak to guard me from
My Foes, but for your Majefties Protection.

King. O *Woolfey!* be to me but half fo kind
As I fhall be to thee. *Seymour,* my Father!
The lovely *Seymour,* whom thou toldft me of,
I did devour her Beauties from thy Lips,
And fed my Ears with the delicious Feaft;
But fince I've feen this Wonder of her Sex!
The Charming'ft Creature e're adorn'd the World;
And find her all as far above thy Praifes,
As Heav'n can be beyond Man's frail defcription.

Card. Have you then feen her, Sir?

King. O yes, my *Woolfey!*
And having feen her, guefs, I needs muft be
But wretched without her, or thy affiftance.

Card. This goes as I expected.   [*Afide.*

King. Help thy Prince!
Why art fo flow? Has *Woolfey* loft his Courage?
That Wit that Emperours and Popes has fway'd——
So, let thy Brain begin to travel now;
Bring forth thou more than King; thou more than Man;
Thou haft a Mine within that fubtle Breaft,
The Stone which dull Philofophy has toyl'd
In vain for——Make me Mafter of thy *Indies*——
Lend me thy Wit to purchafe *Seymour* for me.

Card. You have the Means already in your hands,
Power is the greateft Charmer of that Sex.

King. Command my Power, my Kingdoms to thy aid,
Join to thy Foxes Tail my Lions Skin;
Take thou my Scepter, bind it to thy Crofs,
And to thy Mitre add my humble Crown;
'Tis all my *Woolfey's. Woolfey* fhall be King.
I ask but only *Seymour* in Exchange.

Card. You bid too much: Send for her ftreight to Court;
Make her a Marchionefs, or elfe a Dutchefs;
There's hardly now a Woman but will fell
A foolifh Honour that none fees, for that

D   Which

Which makes a Noife and fplendour in the World.

King. How thou deceiv'ft my eager Expectations!
This I have done without fuch rare Advice:
But oh fhe is inflexible to all!
Deaf to the founds of Vanity and Pomp!
And more remorfelefs than a Saint or Hermite.
Her Chaftity cold as the Frozen Stream,
And then as hard, and never to be thaw'd,
As Cryftal Rocks, or Adamantine Quarries:
That oh I fear, had I but what I covet,
The Crown from *Bullen*'s Head, to offer her,
'Twould fcarcely tempt her to thy Prince's Bed.

Card. Then, Sir, I doubt 'tis hardly in my Power
To help you.

King. Ha! falfe and ungrateful Man!
Is that then all the hope your Brain can give me?

Card. It is impoffible, if fhe be Virtuous,
That e're fhe fhou'd be had by Force or Cunning.
Therefore apply this Remedy a while,
Have but a little Patience 'till 'tis Lawful.

King. Traitor and Poifoner of thy Mafter's Reft,
Muft I defpair? Is that thy precious Council?
Did I defcend to ask Advice from Hell?
Confult thy Wicked Oracle for this?
To tell me what is Lawful?

Card. Underftand me.

King. Give me fome hopes, or, by thy damn'd Ambition,
I'le crumble thee to duft; puff thee to nothing:
And make thee lefs and more dejected far
Than the bafe Fellow that begot thee, Prieft.

Card. Hear me but————

King. Why didft thou infect my Breaft,
And with thy venomous Tongue deceive me, worfe
Than the old Serpent that in Paradife
Betray'd the firft of Mankind with a Bait?
So thou, lurking and hid amidft the Charms
Of *Seymour*'s rare and unfufpected Beauties,
Sungft me her Praifes in fuch tempting Words,
That I with ravifht Ears fwallow'd the found,
And never faw the Sting I fuckt in after.

Card.

Card. You will not give me leave t' explain my felf,
Nor yet to give you Remedy.

King. Tell me;
For Remedy I'le have from Heav'n or Hell,
Or I will take thy Blood, thy Scorpions Blood.
And lay it to my Grief till I have eafe.

Card. Your Fury will not let you underftand me:
When I advis'd to ftay till it was Lawful,
At the fame time I meant to let you know
'Twas not a thing fo hard to bring to pafs.

King. Ha! faid again like *Woolfey!* tell me ftreight.
My Soul waits at the Portal of thy Breaft,
To ravifh from thy Lips the welcome News,
E're they have minted into Words thy Thoughts——
Quick, what can lawfully make *Seymour* mine?

Card. Make her your Queen.

King. Make her my Queen!

Card. Yes, Sir.

King. Sure I but dream; what doft thou mean? or how?

Card. Inveft her Head with *Anna Bullen's* Crown.

King. Sure thou art mad, and would make me fo too——
What, whilft fhe lives?

Card. Ay, whilft fhe lives I faid:
Is that fo ftrange a thing that ne're was done?
Divorce her.

King. Ha!

Card. What is't that makes you ftart?
Divorce her, and take *Seymour* to your Bed.

King. How! take good heed what 'tis thou pull'ft upon
Thy felf——Divorce my lawful virtuous Wife
Without a Caufe!

Card. There is a Caufe.

King. What is't?

Card. Pretend Remorfe of Confcience.

King. Gods!

Card. Ne're wonder:
Say you are troubled and difturb'd within.

King. Eternal Villain! *Lucifer* the Damn'd.   [*Afide.*
Traitor, at what?

Card. At that which feiz'd your Mind,

When

When *Katherine* you divorc'd for *Anna Bullen.*
Confcience! Confcience!

King. Horrid tormenting Fiend!   [*Afide.*
Thou know'ft fhe was my Brother's Wife, and *Bullen*
On no fuch juft pretence I can difclaim.

Card. No matter; on the like diftruft of Confcience
That made you do the one, you may the other.
Give out that fhe's not lawfully your Wife,
The firft alive, and that you never had
A Difpenfation from his Holinefs.

King. His Holinefs! I'm blafted with the thoughts:
Pernicious Traitor! How can this be done?

Card. Leave it to me; Confent you, 'tis enough:
And I'le engage, on forfeit of my life,
To get a Licence from our Holy Father
To difanul this Marriage, and to take
Into your lawful Bed the Beauteous *Seymour.*

King. But then I ftill remain unfreed from *Katherine.*

Card. The Church fhall grant a Difpenfation too
For that.

King. What Horrour's this I hear! Can this be true?
In all my wanton and luxurious Youth,
Or in my blackeft thoughts of Luft and Rage,   [*Afide.*
I ne're yet found one Wifh amongft them all,
Of fuch a deep Infernal hue. The Horrour
Has kindled my whole Blood into a Flame,
And made me blufh a deeper Scarlet than
This Villain's Robe. Difloyal wicked Monfter!
But I will ftrive to hide my juft Refentments.
Divorce my fecond Wife without a Caufe!   [*To him.*
Could it be done, what would the Nation fay?
What would the Action look like but a Hell;
To warn fucceeding Princes from the like,
And blot me from the Scrole of Pious Kings:
Could it be lawful *Wooſſey*, I would hearken.

Card. Then lawful it fhall be in fpight of Scruples:
I fee your Confcience is an Infant grown,
A Child again, and wants to be inftructed——
Come, let me lead you by the hand, and point
A way for you to walk on even ground:

So fafe, the niceft Confcience fhall commend
And choofe it.

King. Now thou doft rejoice thy Prince.

Card. What if fhe be unfaithful to your Bed,
And prov'd fo?

King. Ha! there's Thunder in that word,
The Bolt ran through, and fhiver'd me to pieces.
Difloyal to my Bed! Adultrous! Hah!
Saidft thou not fo? Yet hold, if this be true,
There hangs a Shower of Cordial in my reach
To cure this horrid Fit. *Woolfey*, beware
How thou doft dally with my hopes and fears;
Look to't, and fee you wrong her not; for if
Thou doft, by all the Plagues thy Soul deferves,
All Hell fhall be too little for thy Carkafs:
New Hells fhall be created, and more hot
Than what's prepar'd for Traitors, Parracides,
For Ravifhers of Mothers, luftful Nuns,
For *Lucifer* himfelf t'endure; nay more
Than Villain, Pope, or Cardinal ever felt.
Speak how thou know'ft it. Quick.

Card. Alas! my Lord,
I never meant it enter'd in my own
Particular Knowledge: but it is Reported.

King. Reported, faid'ft thou! Is not that enough?
Report! why fhe is damn'd, if fhe's but thought
A Whore, much more reported to be fo.
'Tis not the act alone that wrongs thy King;
Each Smile, each Glance, and every wanton Look,
That's meant t'another, if I leave unpunifh'd,
Shall brand me with the ignominious Name
Of *Wittal*, which is worfe——make me but fure
That the leaft Breath has utter'd fuch a found,
Or whifper'd to the air that fhe's Unchafte,
By all the horrid Fiends that punifh Luft,
And by the black Concupifcence of Hell,
I'le tumble her from the Throne into a Dungeon——
Name me the Man that is fufpected.

Card. Piercy.

King. Piercy!

Card. Yes, Sir: He is the Man ſhe dotes on;
'Tis he lies deeper in her Breaſt than ever;
For him ſhe ſighs, and hoards up all her Wiſhes;
Gives him her Perſon warm, inſpir'd with Paſſion,
Whilſt for your ſelf ſhe only treats you with
The cold dead Body of departed Love.

King. Is *Piercy* then at Court?

Card. He is this Day
Arriv'd.

King. Hough! Come without my leave ſay'ſt thou?

Card. He is, no doubt to conſummate their Joyes,
Their Signs and Tokens to compare, which they
By Letters and Devices in their abſence
Have hourly plotted to deceive you, Sir;
And put in practice when the time is ripe.

King. Hell and tormenting Furies——I believe thee.

Card. Nay in your Bed and in her Dreams ſhe thinks on't;
When Pleaſures made you dull, it whetted her——

King. Hold, I can hear no more. By all my Wrongs
And cheated Hopes, thou bring'ſt to my Remembrance,
How all Complaiſances to me were dragg'd
And forc'd from her, like Mirth from one in Torture!
Sometimes I found her Face all drown'd in Tears,
With Gales of Sighs juſt blowing off thoſe Storms,
In fear away: Sometimes again in Bluſhes,
As if then all the wanton Heat of love
Were darting through her Eyes to meet my Flame;
But when with eager haſte I catch'd her in
Theſe Arms and preſt her Lips, alack I found
Inſtead of Summer there no Ice ſo cold;
Inſtead of breath that wou'd revive the dead,
No Air ſo chill, nor Winter Blaſt ſo keen.

Card. Thus all her actions ſtill will be to you:
The Roſes of her Bloom ſhe keeps for him,
The Thorns for you——Had you been *Piercy* then!

King. Let me embrace the Saver of his Prince,
The dear Preſerver of my Life and Honour!
What ſhall I do for thee, my Friend?

Re-enter

Re-enter Rochford.

Card. **Here's** *Rochford!*
Pray fmooth your Brow, and hide your Difcontent:
And now y' are going to the Queen fmile on her.
Mean while fhe'll ftumble, like a hafty Child,
And act more plain and open to your Juftice;
And when you find her tripping, on the fudden
Strike like the Hand of Heav'n, a fure Revenge,
And never let her rife again.
   King. I will————
My Lord, you may come near: Where is the Queen ? [*To* Roch.
   Roch. I left her in the Drawing-Room.
   King. Ah *Woolfey*!
What Angel e're fo bright as Woman was,
Had not the firft fcorn'd her Creator's Laws;
For neareft his own likenefs they were made,
'Till they by falfenefs did their Sex degrade. [*Exeunt* K.& Card.
                                        [*Manet* Rochford.

   Roch. What means this fudden alteration !

Enter Piercy.

Is not that *Piercy*? Oh! too true he comes !
Not like a joyful Bridgroom, as was told thee,
Poor cheated Sifter ! but like one, alas!
That knows already, the bafe wrongs our Friends
Have heap'd upon him ! where fhall I avoid him ?
Ah! why muft I of all the Plot be Curft ?
To look upon a Face fo full of horror ;
That like a Hell, at once upbraids my Guilt,
And lafhes me with the Remembrance ?
   Pier. Methinks I walk like one that's in a Dream,
A horrid Dream, and fain would be awake!
Thefe Rooms of State look not as they were wont,
When *Anna Bullen* oft has run to meet me ;
But feem like Fairy-Land, a Wildernefs.
My Friends, like Beafts that never yet faw Man,
Start at my fight ; and fhun me worfe than Fire.

What

What mean you Heavens! what mean thofe boding **Vifions** !
O that fome Friend, fome Friend indeed would meet me !
And wake me out of it——Behold ; 'tis granted————
Is not that *Rochford* there ? my Deareft Brother *!*————

    Roch. My Lord, my *Piercy* !

    Pier. Come thou to my Armes.——
Methinks th' art not concern'd to fee thy Friend :
When I embrace thee, 'tis a pain I find,
Thy Friendfhip is as cold as Winter Blafts,
Or as chill Age is to a tender Virgin !
What ails my Friend ? fay quickly.

    Roch. Nothing ails me.

    Pier. Nothing ! why look'ft thou then fo full of horrour?
Thy down-caft Eyes call to my fad remembrance,
How paffing by yon Gallery of Pictures,
That happy Gallery that was once the Scene
Of many a joyful meeting with thy Sifter !
Looking with wonder on thofe famous Perfons,
Whom the rare Painter had with fo much Art
Defcrib'd, to make Pofterity amends,
For their bright Forms now moulder'd in their Urns ;
With their Immortal Shapes of Beauty here ;
There as we us'd to walk, none e're fo kind,
With loving Arms and tender Wifhes join'd,
A glad remembrance in their Looks we fpy'd,
Of what their Bodies had on Earth enjoy'd ;
With ftedfaft Eyes they watch'd us all the while,
And when we fmil'd, they would be fure to fmile.
Or if we chanc'd to weep and figh our woe,
They feem'd to pity us, and do fo too :
Such fympathy they drew from all our Fears,
Our very Griefs, and every Look was theirs.

    Roch. The over-flowing of your Love-fick Fancy.

    Pier. But mark me now, my *Rochford* ; mind the fad
Cataftrophe.   They lookt not now like Friends
Of Comfort, but like boding *Sybils* rather ;
Their Smiles converted all to darting Frowns,
Whilft with their feeming Voice and Hands, methought,
They chid and beckon'd me to fhun the place,
As if they did intend to fay aloud,

                                  Ah

Ah *Piercy!* 'tis not now as heretofore,
Piercy begone, for thou fhalt happy be no more.
Roch. Ah, my Lord!
Pier. Ha! what fay'ft thou? 'tis enough,
There hangs a dreadful Tale upon thy Brow,
And there's fome horrid meaning in that word———
Let thy dire Looks fpeak all the reft, I prithee;
Th' haft pierc'd quite through me like an Ague-Fit,
Stopt every circling paffage of my Blood,
And made me fweat big drops as cold as Ice———
Say quick! How fares thy Sifter? is fhe well?
My Love! my Wife! Did I not call her Wife?
Speak, Is fhe living? Is fhe dead? If fo,
And thou dar'ft utter it! plant thy dread Voice
Juft like a Cannon to thy *Piercy's* Breaft,
And fhiver me to pieces.
Roch. By thefe words
I find he knows not of my Sifter's Marriage!   [*Afide.*
Still worfe and worfe!———Alas! my Lord, fhe lives!   [*To* Pier.
Pier. Lives! oh the joy! But is fhe ought than well?
Tell it with fpeed! why didft thou fay, alas?
Roch. Well fhe is too.
Pier. Then bleffed be that Voice;
But why thou fpeak'ft it with fuch cold referve,
I cannot guefs.   Oh tell it out with joy!
Tell it aloud with fhouting to the Spheres,
That they may eccho with glad Harmony:
Thy Sifter lives: my *Bullen* is in health.
Roch. She is in health: but———
Pier. Ha! but what? fpeak out:
Why doft thou torture me with dire fufpence?
If there be any thing can now be call'd Misfortune,
When thy dear Sifter is in health, out with it;
Let it be worfe than Thunder I can bear it.
Roch. Alas! kind *Piercy* force not me to tell you,
Too foon you'l hear the News from one perhaps
That can relate it, Rocky as he is,
Without a Sigh or Tear in pity of you.
Pier. You Heav'nly Pow'rs! What does my *Rochford* mean!
Methinks the joyful Tidings in my Breaft,

E   That

That she's in health, does chide me for my Fears;
But then again a fatal heaviness
Streight intercepts this dawn of Comfort there,
And like a Cloud hides all those new-born Beams
Of Hope, and bids me dread I know not what.
I am in Hell, in Torments, worse, in Doubt——
Is there no Balsom that can cure this Sting?
No *Oedipus* that can unfold this Riddle?
I prithee, gentle *Rochford*, do not rack me:
Take off this heavy Weight that sinks thy Brother.
Come, flatter me, if thou'rt affraid to tell
The Truth, and say that all these killing words
Were not in Earnest.

Enter Northumberland.

Roch. See, your Father's here.
Pier. He will take pity, and release me sure.
North. *Harry*, thou art most welcome to thy Father;
Welcome to all, and welcome to the King.
Rejoice, my Son, and deck thy Face with Smiles:
There's Love and Fortune coming toward thee.
　Pier. Pardon me, best of Fathers! spare my Answer: [*Kneels.*
Oh tell me first what News is from my Love?
How does my Mistress fare? and what's become
Of Beauteous *Anna Bullen?* quickly, Sir.
　North. Why, what's become of her? She's very well.
What should become of her? She's Marry'd, Son.
　Pier. Marry'd!
　North. Marry'd! ay Marry'd, that she is!
A Queen she's too, a joyful Queen, I tell thee.
　Pier. Marry'd! and to the King! by all my hopes,
By all our chast, eternal Vows of Love
It cannot be, although my Father says it;
You, whom I'le credit sooner than an Angel.
Marry'd! my *Anna Bullen* false, and Marry'd!
Perswade me that the Sun has lost its Virtue,
The Earth, the teeming Earth, forgot to bear,
That Nature shall be Nature now no more;
That all the Elements shall vanish streight,

Turn

Turn to Confufion, into Chaos fhrink,
And you, and I, and all the living World,
Are what we were before we were begot;
All this muft be, when *Anna Bullen's* falfe.

North. I tell thee, rafh and difobedient Boy,
Marry'd fhe is without fuch Miracles.

Pier. Ah, deareft Father, on my Knees I beg you,
Repeat that horrid, difmal word no more;
To be obedient, and at once to hear
My Miftrefs wrong'd, is not in *Piercy's* power.
Here, crufh this Infect, pound me into Duft,
I'm at your Foot! oh lay it on my Neck,
And punifh me with death, ten thoufand deaths;
For whilft I live I muft be guilty ftill,
And near can think that *Anna Bullen's* falfe:
O Sir, be merciful and juft at once,
And fay you did it but to try your *Piercy.*

North. Rife, and repent, and do not tempt my Anger,
Which thou fhould'ft feel, but that I pity thee,
And think thy Folly Punifhment enough.

Pier. See, Sir, her Brother's more concern'd than I
To hear fuch words. Come, tell 'em, deareft *Rochford,*
Proclaim her Virtue loud as Cherubins,
Tell 'em, thefe Rocks, they may in time relent,
And hear the fad Complaints of injur'd Honour:
Is fhe not Chaft! Chaft as the Virgin light,
And conftant as the Turtle to its Mate,
Her Perfon facred ftill to all Mankind,
And Beauties lefs corrupted, lefs defil'd,
Than is the lovely Blew that fragrant hangs
On *Autumn* Fruit, or Morning Dew on Rofes.

North. Tell him, my Lord.

Pier. Oh hear the Charming found;
Tell 'em, and undeceive 'em, Friend; tell 'em
How thou wert by, when firft we plighted Troths,
And fwore Eternal Faith, Eternal Love,
By every Saint, and every Star that fhone,
Who then look'd down as joyful Witneffes,
And darted forth in all their bright Array,
To fee our Loves that fhin'd more bright than they.

Gent.

Gent. My Lord, the King and Queen are paffing by.

North. Look you, Romantick Sir, behold your Miftrefs,
Whofe Bride fhe is.

[*King and Queen, Lords and Ladies pafs over the Stage,*
    Northumberland *follows the King.*

Pier. By the Immortal Powers that gave me life,
And Eyes and Senfes to believe, 'tis fhe————
It is the King, and *Anna Bullen* Crown'd!
Why Father, *Rochford*, Friends, is it not fo?
And did fhe not like haughty *Juno* walk?
Who, as fhe held the Thunderer by the hand,
Lookt down with fcorn on the low World, from whence
She came; fo did fhe caft a loathing Eye
Upon the place where humble *Piercy* ftands————
Now you are mute, dumb as thofe Conjurations
You hir'd juft now from Hell to be my Ruine;
Ha! is't not fo? Confefs that it is fo,
And I am bleft; own it, and make poor *Piercy* happy.

Roch. Alas! my Lord; afflict your mind no more,
'Tis torment to your Friend to fee you thus.

Pier. Friend, fay'ft thou? I difclaim that Name in all,
In Father, Brother, Sifter, and Companion;
Nature her felf abhors it, like the Plague,
And banifhes that Gueft from all her Creatures————
Falfe Brother to the falfeft Woman living!
Was it for this that I was fent from Court?
Was it for this the fubtleft of her Sex
Sent me a Letter with ten thoufand Charms,
To let me know that I fhould write, and fhould
Be written to no more till my return?
T' avoid fufpition, as fhe faid; but 'twas
To flatter me that I fhould not miftruft her.

Roch. By Heav'n, and all that's true, fhe's not to blame.

Pier. Here, *Rochford*, rip, and tear her from my heart,
Faft rooted as fhe is: The Poifon fwells,
O lance it with thy Sword, and give me eafe:
She's Hell! fhe's worfe! fhe's Madnefs to the Brain;
I am poffeft, and carry an Hoft of Devils:
For he that wears a perjur'd Woman here,
Has in his Breaft ten thoufand Fiends to fcourge him.

                                                    Re-enter

Re-enter Northumberland.

North. Come, my beſt Son, the King Salutes thee, *Piercy*;
Come, ſee the Bride he has prepar'd for thee,
And think no more of *Anna Bullen* now.
   Pier. Ha! bring me to her ſtreight! Is ſhe a Woman?
A bright diſſembling and proteſting Woman?
Smooth as the ſmiling pittileſs Ocean is by fits;
But then her Heart as Rocky, deep, and fathomleſs:
Has ſhe a Face as tempting as the fair
Deceitful Fruit of *Sodom*, but when taſted,
Is rottenneſs and horrour to the Core?
Is ſhe ſo kind, that nothing can be kinder?
Nay were ſhe *Anna Bullen* all without,
And *Bullen* all within, I'd marry her
To be reveng'd!
   North. Thou doſt rejoice thy Father:
She is as good and beautiful as Angels,
And has ten thouſand Pounds a year; which added
To thy Eſtate, will make you far more happy
Than *Harry* with his Crown, or *Anna Bullen.*
   Pier. Come, bring me to her: when ſhall we be marry'd
   North. When my Son pleaſes: If thou wilt, to Morrow.
   Pier. To Morrow! Now: To Morrow is too late:
What muſt I waſte a Day, and loſe a Smile!
The King with *Bullen* revels all this while.
Haſte, thou ſlow Sun! when wilt thou bring the Morn?
And when! oh when ſhall the long Day be worn!
That theſe triumphant Arms may ſeize my Bride,
And claſp her gently like a wanton Tide.
In Floods of Extaſies I'le drown; and ſay,
Thus *Harry* and his Queen live all the day;
Thus he embraces her all o're, and o're;
Whilſt for each Kiſs I'le reap a thouſand more:
And for each Pleaſure they ſhall act that Night
I'le pattern then, and double with delight:
But for that rareſt Bliſs we bluſh to own,
Spite and Revenge much more my Joys ſhall Crown. [*Exeunt.*

The End of the Second Act.

ACT III. SCENE I.

Enter Cardinal and Blunt feverally.

Card. HAIL to the Sacred Queen of Wit and Beauty;
　　　Hail to the Emprefs of the World that fhould be.
Blunt. What News? What Song of Comfort brings my *Woolfey?*
Methinks your Looks fhine like the Sun of Joy,
And Smiles, more glittering than your Robe, appear:
Come, for I long to be partaker of it———
Say, is it Great? Shall *Bullen* fink to Hell?
Shall this proud Exhalation vanifh ftreight?
Or, fhall fhe ftill be Queen t'affront my *Woolfey?*
　　Card. No: I'd firft pawn both Body and Soul to Hell,
For but a Dram of Poyfon that would kill
The Heretick.
　　Blunt. Oh famous *Cardinal!*
Rome's Sacred Champion, and the Saints of *Rome!*
What can reward thee but the Mytre here,
And when th'art dead, a mighty Throne, as high
As was great *Lucifer's* before his fall?
　　Card. Have I not liv'd more fplendid than the King?
More aw'd and famous than was *Harry* ftill?
Have I not fcatter'd with a Liberal Hand,
And fow'd more Seed to Charity, than all
The Kingdom elfe? Built fuch vaft Palaces,
As neither *Italy* nor *Rome* can pattern?
Which *England's* Monarchs have been proud to dwell in.
　　Blunt. And but for thee, the Nation had been fcorn'd.
　　Card. Who fram'd fuch fumptuous Embaffies, as I,
With fuch a Glorious Train of Servants deck'd,
As *Germany* and *France* both wonder'd at,
And thought that all the Nation follow'd me;
Whilft *Tudor* here, as a lefs King than I,
Was ferv'd, but with the gleanings of my Pomp?
　　Blunt. 'Twas *Woolfey,* our Great Mafter's greater Servant,
who, as he rode to meet the Emperour,

Ere

Ere he approach'd, firſt chec'd his pamper'd Steed,
And ſtood at diſtance to receive that Monarch;
Whilſt *Maximilian,* as became him beſt,
Firſt did unlight, and firſt embrac'd my *Woolſey.*
 Card. And have not I rul'd *Harry* and the Nation
Shall then this ſtrong Foundation of my Greatneſs
Be undermin'd by ſuch a Wretch as *Bullen !*
By the weak practice of a ſpleenful Woman !
A thing, that I have made ; a Poppet-Queen,
Dreſt up by me, to Act her Scene of Greatneſs,
And all her Motions guided by this Hand!
 Blunt. Shall ſhe then Mount the Fame to ruine *Woolſey ?*
 Card. No ; by my Self, that moment ſhe attempts it,
She pulls a dreadful Tower upon her Head ;
When I begin to totter, if I muſt,
Like a huge Oak, that's leaning o're a Wall,
I'le take my Aim, and cruſh her with my fall ——
Piercy's arriv'd, there's Aid for your Revenge.
 Blunt. I heard ſo, and perceiv'd it by the Queen.
 Card. By that ſhe has diſcover'd the deceit,
And finds him Innocent, now 'tis too late ;
This makes her careleſs, to her own undoing ;
For when the Amorous King comes, loaded with
Big hopes, and thinks to take his fill of Joys,
Streight, like the ſenſitive, nice Plant that ſhrinks,
And on a ſudden gathers up its Leaves,
When 'tis but touch'd, ſhe will contract her Charms
And ſhut 'em from him in her ſullen Boſom,
As cold as Winter to his warm Embraces :
This, when the vext and paſſionate King perceives,
He'll hate, and caſt her from him in a Rage.
 Blunt. See ! yonders *Rochford* coming towards us.
Big with glad Looks, I hope, to be deliver'd
Of ſomething that will forward our Deſign.
 Card. I will retire, and leave him to your Care,
To mannage him with all the Art of Woman ;
And Hell, if Heaven wont, inſpire your Wit
And Malice.   *Ex.* Card.

               Enter

Enter Rochford.

Roch. Brighteft of thy dazling Sex,
That wears the Charms of all the World about thee;
How have I been this long, long hour in pain,
In Torments and in Darknefs all the while!
Sun of my Joy, to wafte the tedious Day,
And Star to gaze the live-long-night away.
   Blunt. O, you are grown a Courtier now indeed,
My Lord; but 'tis no wonder now, you are
Exalted, and are Brother to the Queen:
'Tis hard for one to gain a look from you,
Without the purchafe of————I will not tell you——
   Roch. Ha! Brother to the Queen! to *Jupiter*:
And if my ravifh'd Senfe deceives me not,
I will not change my State to fhine in Heaven!
To be the darling Brother of the Sun,
Qr one of *Leda*'s Twins that deck the Sky:
No, *Caftor* I defie thee.
   Blunt. Hold, my Lord;
I will not chide you, though you have deferv'd it:
For all thofe Raptures are but ftarts in Love,
And feldom hold out to the Races end;
Or elfe like Straw that gives a fudden blaze,
And foon is out.
   Roch. Oh fay not fo, my Goddefs!
The *Negro*, neareft Neighbour to the Sun,
That lives under the torrid burning Line,
Feels not the warmth that does poffefs my Breaft.
And, oh forgive the vaft Comparifon,
Hell's flame is not fo vehement or lafting.
   Blunt. Enough, my Lord: I'le put you to your Trial:
Prepare, and fee how well you can obey;
But that you may not ftrive without all hope,
Like Slaves condemn'd for ever to the Gallies;
Here is my Hand, an Earneft of my Promife,
That as I find you Faithful, I'le Reward you.
   Roch. Your Hand! where am I! tell me, God of Love!
   Blunt. But mark me: Hear, as from a Prophet, this:

Be fure you merit well this firft of Favours,
And keep the Oath you vow upon this Hand,
Elfe I'le denounce a worfe than Hell fhall follow
Your Sacrilegious Crime.

Roch. Lo, here I fwear——
But tell me, Heav'n! what fignifies an Oath!
When 'tis impoffible I fhould be falfe?
I fwear upon this Altar, breathing Incenfe!
Eternal Love! Eternal Conftancy——
Divineft, fofteft——Sweeteft——   [*Kiffes her Hand.*

Blunt. Go my Lord.
And now you have it, brag to my undoing;
For never any but your King can boaft
The like.

Roch. And he, th' unworthieft of Mankind,
Who having fuch a Jewel in his Breaft,
The Crown not half fo Sacred, were it mine,
To fell it for a falfe and glittering Trifle:
So filly *Indians* barter Gold and Pearls
For Baubles.

Blunt. What your Sifter, treach'rous Man!
You do not mean it; nor can I endure
To hear her fo degraded; if 'twere real:
Sh' has Goodnefs, and has Beauties more than I,
And merits what fhe does poffefs, a Crown:
And much the more, becaufe fhe fought not for it;
Which is the caufe, I fear, that fhe's unhappy——
You vifit her, not only as a Brother,
But as a Friend, and Partner of her Councils;
You love like Twins, like Lovers, or indeed
As a fond Brother, and kind Sifter fhould.
How bears fhe this unwelcome State? or rather,
How does fhe brook the Wrong that's done to *Piercy?*

Roch. All her Reflections on it ftreight will vanifh;
A King and Crown are Charms invincible;
No Storms, nor Difcontents can long abide,
Where Love and Empire plead: but foon will flye,
Scatter'd like Mifts before the Sun of Power.

Blunt. You fpeak indifferently, my Lord, and like

Miftruft of her you Love: I long to hear
The more what you would fain difguife from me————
Have you fo foon forgot the Oath you took?
Or is't fo lately, that you think 'tis fcarce
Reach'd down to Hell, to claim you Perjur'd there?
Or think you that I e're can hate the Sifter,
When with a blufh I own, I love the Brother?
Falfe and ungrateful Man! farewell.

    Roch. O ftay!
Rip open my Bofom to my naked Heart,
And read what-e're you think is written there.
Had I no Tongue to fpeak, I'd fuffer that,
Rather than once deny you any thing.

    Blunt. He foftens, turns, and changes, as I'd have him; [*Afide.*
His Waxen Soul begins to melt apace:
He is my Slave, my Chain'd and Gally Slave:
Oh that I had but *Harry* fo to torture!
But I'le Revenge my felf on this foft Fool,
On *Bullen,* and on all their Race at once
That were the Curfed caufe of my undoing.
You find my Paffion and good Nature quickly,   [*To* Roch.
That makes you ufe me thus.

    Roch. Ten thoufand Pardons————
    Blunt. No more; I can forgive, if you deferve it;
I charge you, as a Sign of your Repentance,
Go vifit ftreight the Queen, and *Piercy* too;
You hear he's come to Court; and what you learn
From them, that ought concerns their former Loves,
From time to time, acquaint me with the Story,
And you fhall lock the fecret in my Breaft,
As fafe, as in your own.

    Roch. 'Twere Blafphemy
But to fufpect it.

    Blunt. I require this of you;
Not that I doubt the Virtue of the Queen,
But know, that, worfe than Hell, I hate the King,
(To which juft hatred 'tis you owe my Love)
And wifh your Sifter, and all Humane kind,
Would hate him too.

    Roch. I'le inftantly obey you.

                                 Blunt.

Blunt. Come back, my Lord; this readiness has charm'd me:
And now I can't but give you some kind hopes——
You may have leave to visit me hereafter.
And talk of Love, perhaps I'le take it kindly.
Roch. Blest Harmony! Happiest of Mankind, I.
Blunt. And you may write to me, and best by Proxy:
For tho the King not visits me, as he was wont,
Yet he is Jealous——.
Let all your Amorous Letters be disguis'd,
Under the borrow'd Name of Brother still,
Directed to me by the stile of Sister.
Roch. In all things I'le obey my lovely Goddess!
Blunt. These Papers once shall be of Consequence.   [*Aside.*
See, the Queen comes, her Soul in discontent,   [*To* Roch.
And longs to be disburthen'd.   I will leave you——
A fit occasion's offer'd,   now she's on
The Rack, to ease her by a fond Confession.   [*Ex.* Blunt.

Enter Queen *and Ladies.*

Queen. Where am I now ?——My Brother ! Is it you?
I hear that *Piercy's* come to Court.
Roch. He is.
Queen. Where shall I hide my guilty Face from him?
And shut me where he ne're may see me more?
For now I start at every humane Shape,
And think I meet wrong'd *Piercy* in my way,
Like one escap'd for Murther, in his Flight
Shuns every Beast, and Trembles at the Wind,
And thinks each Bush a Man to apprehend him.——

Enter Diana.

I sent thee to the Queen, *Diana,* say,
How fares she in her hopeless, lost Estate?
What Answer bring'st thou, that is Death to hear?
Come talk of Misery, and fill my Breast
With Woe: I'le lay my Ears to the sad sound,
And thence Extract it as the Bees do Hony,
Grief is the Food that the afflicted live by——

F 2   Talk

Talk any thing; there's nought fo dreadful as
The thoughts of injur'd *Piercy*, in my Breaft.

Dian. The Princefs *Dowager* is dead.

Queen. What Princefs?
Art thou a temporizing falfe one too?
And haft fo foon forgot fhe was thy Queen?

Dian. Queen *Katherine's* dead.

Queen. Alas! then is fhe dead!
Then fhe has got the ftart of *Anna Bullen*———
Came you too late to pay my Duty to her?

Dian. No : for fh' enjoyed her Senfes to the laft,
And then not feem'd to dye, but fall afleep.

Queen. So bold is Innocence, it conquers Death,
And after makes amends for all the wrongs
Suftain'd in Life.

Dian. When I began to tell her,
I came by your command, to make a tender
Of your moft humble Duty, and Condole
Her Majefties Mifortune and Diftemper;
She check'd me at that word, and as you have feen
A clear Sky, with a travelling Cloud o'retook,
And quickly gone, fo fhe put on a Frown,
Which did not laft, and anfwer'd with a Smile :
Why did you fay, your Majefty to me,
She faid, a Name I loath? Go, tell your Queen,
Let her not fix on Greatnefs to be happy,
But take a fad Example here by me :
I, who was Daughter, Niece, and Sifter too,
To three great Emperours, and Wife, alas!
To the moft potent Prince in *Chriftendom*,
Muft Dye more wretched than the meaneft Creature,
In a ftrange Country, 'midft my Enemies,
Not one of all my great Relations here
To pity me, nor Friend to bury me :
And then fhe wept, and turn'd her gentle Face
The other way, and quickly after Dy'd.

Queen. Go on; Why doft thou ceafe this Melody?
Thy Voice exceeds the mourning *Philomels*;
The dying Swan takes not that pleafure in
Her note, as I in fuch Celeftial Mufick:

Haft

Haft thou no more of it?
Come play the Artift: Shew thou to my Fancy,
Th' Infernal Paths that lead to Infinite Horror;
Op'n all the Charnel Houfes of the Dead,
And fright away, if it be poffible,
The fad Remains of injur'd *Piercy* here.

Enter King.

[Exeunt Diana and Rochford.

King. Yonder fhe is, in Tears amidft her Glories!
You lavifh Stars, what will content this Scorner?
From a mean Spring I took this fhining Pebble,
And plac'd her in my Heart, and in my Crown,
The faireft and the beft lov'd Jewel there:
And fate her on my Throne to be ador'd:
Yet fhe contemns all this, and would do more,
The Heavens are all too narrow for her Soul!
Gods, you muft flatter and defcend to her,
Or fhe'll not ftir one jot to you——She is
So very proud.
  Queen. My Lord.
  King. Sit down again,
I but difturb you; therefore I'le return;
For fure they muft be tender thoughts, for which
You pay fuch lavifh Tribute from your Eyes.
  Queen. Sir, I was thinking of th' uncertain State
Of Greatnefs, and amongft its fad Misfortunes,
What would become of me, alas! if you
(Which I've no reafon to fufpect)
Should change your Love; and that produc'd thefe Tears.
  King. Y'are in the right, if that fhould ever happen;——
But what begets fuch Doubts within your Breaft?
You have done nothing to deferve fuch fears:
You love me, and as long as that fhall laft,
Miftruft not *Harry.*
  Queen. By my hopes I do.
  King. Bleft found. I will hear nothing but my *Bullen:*
Woolfey and Devil tempt me now no more!   [*Afide.*
Then fhake thefe Clouds of forrow from thy Eyes,
And dart thy brighter Beams, like *April* Sun-fhine,

Into

Into my Bofom, and thus lock me ever——
Oh, now I nought remember but thy Charms,
And quite forget what-e're I was before.
One word of Blifs, one word of Softnefs from thee,
To banifh hence Sufpitions, like the Plague,
And clear our Breafts from jealoufies for ever——
What, not a fyllable do I deferve?
Thefe Kiffes, faint Embraces, and thefe Odours,
Are ravifh'd, not-beftow'd upon me——ha!

 Queen. What means my Lord?

 King. What means the Traiterous *Bullen?*
By Heav'n fhe wants the cunning Trick and Skill;
The eafie quick Delufion of her Sex,
To hide her falfenefs——By all Hell fhe's damn'd.

 Queen. O Gracious Sir.

 King. Too gracious not to kill thee——
For whom, for whom are your kind Looks referv'd?
Hide you your Minion; for his fafeguard, do.
For were he 'mongft his happy Stars, I'd reach him.
I'm frightful as a Ghoft, or a Difeafe:
For when I think to hold her in thefe Arms,
She ftruggles like the Quarry in the Toil:
And yields her felf unto my loath'd Embraces,
With fuch a forc'd and awker'd willingnefs,
As men, when they are paft all hopes of life,
Refign themfelves into the power of Death.

 Queen. What Fiend has put fuch Thoughts into your Breaft?
When did I wrong you? How have I been falfe?
Yet I will not complain againft my Lord.
Since 'tis your Will——Sir, have I not obey'd you?
No Slave fo humbly faithful to your Pleafures,
And in your Bed, with blufhing, paid thofe Duties
That modeft Virgin, or chaft Wife could do:
And if I was not wanton, pray forgive me.

 King. Yes, yes, I have your outfide; but Hell knows,
And thy falfe felf, who 'tis enjoys thy Soul!
You yield to me indeed, 'tis true: but moft
Unwillingly you part with your dear Sweets,
Unlefs it be to him that has your Hoard,
But guard your fatal Honey with a Sting

Gainft

Gainſt thoſe you hate————Your Perſon you reſign,
But as to Priſon; my Arms are but the Grates
Through which your Mind is longing ſtill to be abroad :
Nay in the very Moment of Enjoyment :
And who would think but then I ſhould be happy?
There's ſtill another's Picture in your Heart,
On which you look, and fanſie I am He,
And all the while I'm ſporting for another.

 Queen. Can Heav'n hear this! O cruel, faithleſs Lord.
 King. No: to thy *Syren's* Voice I'le ſtop my Ears;
A thouſand times, like them, th'haſt cheated me,
Laid my juſt Paſſion to a gentle Calm,
VVhilſt Storms behind were ready to devour me.
On thy falſe dangerous Charms I'le wrack no more,
But ſeek for ſhelter on ſome kinder Shore;
A grateful Beauty here ſhall reign alone,
And chace thee from my Heart, and from thy Throne.
Ha! who comes there? My gentle *Woolſey* come,
And with thy Counſel ſtreight defend my Breaſt.

   [*The King meets* Woolſey, *and goes out leaning on him.*
 Queen. Did not my Lord flye from me in a rage,
Arm'd with a Frown, and darted it quite through me?
And *Woolſey* in his Favourites place again?
Nay, then the Wonder is expir'd; that proud,
That great bad man, and *Lucifer,* ne're meant
Me nor my Virtue well————The King's Inconſtancy
Begins to ſhew its *Janus* Face again :
And all the Doubts of an Unhappy Wretch,
My Fears by Day, and horrid Dreams by Night,
Are come to paſs.

Enter Piercy.

 Pier. What ſhall I fear to ſee her !
And tell her Face to Face the Perjuries
And Falſeneſs that ſh' has heap'd upon her Soul,
And ruin'd mine? ————Lo, where the Falſe one is!
In counterfeited Grief? By Heav'n in Tears !
As if her ſins already did upbraid her !

Juſt

Juft Pow'rs ! can you behold a Form fo fair,
And fuffer Falfenefs to inhabit there ?
The Morning Sun rifen from its Watry Bed,
Lefs precious drops does on *Arabia* fhed :
And facred Viols of rich *April*-Showers ;
When he alternate Rain and Sun-fhine pours ;
Nor is he half fo Beautiful and Gay,
As fhe a wiping of thofe Tears away.

    Queen. Ha, *Piercy* ! I'm betray'd. Advife me Heav'n !
What fhall I do !——Begone, this place is Hell ;
Vipers and Adders lurking under Smiles,
And flatt'ring Cloths of State : Oh! do not tread here ;
Under this Mask of Gallantry and Beauty,
Is a rude Wild ; nay, worfe, a dangerous Ocean,
Into whofe Jaws, Love, like a Calenture,
Will tempt us, where we both muft Sink and Perifh.

    Pier. What, can fo mean a Creature fright a Queen !
Behold a wretched Thing of your undoing.

    Queen. See where he ftands, the Mark of pity, Heav'n !
Shut, fhut thy Eyes, and fly with fpeed away ;
Or view the Rocks and Quick-fands, if thou ftay,
Left this rough *Hellifpont* I venture on,
And like *Leander* tempt my Fate, and drown.—— [*Ex.* Queen.

    Pier. Ha! fhe's furpriz'd! fhuns me! and flies from me!
And more affrighted is at *Piercy*'s wrongs,
Than Guilty Ghofts, that having fcap'd to Earth,
Hear the Cock Crow to fummon 'em away,
And ftart and tremble at the fight of Day.
But yet fhe look'd not like a Foe upon me ;
And as fhe parted, told me with her Eyes,
That there was fomething in thofe fpeaking Tears,
Which might Excufe her, and Condemn her *Piercy.*

Enter Northumberland.

    North. Son, I am come to tell you joyful News,
The King has Charm'd the fair *Diana* for thee,
And is refolv'd to Marry her to morrow,
And Celebrate the Nuptials with a Pomp.

    Pier. The King ! the King is Marry'd, Sir.

North. He is.

But thou art not: H' intends to give her to thee
Himfelf: Why doft thou ftart? 'Twas but this day
You Swore and Vow'd, with all the Signs of Joy,
And Duty to your Father, you'd obey me.

Pier. Alas! I did: But cannot Heav'n, nor you
Forgive a rafh, unhappy Man his Vow?

North. No: by the Blood that Honours *Piercy's* Veins,
I fwear, I will not———
For Marry'd thou fhalt be, and that to her,
Or live a Vagabond, banifh'd from Wealth,
From Friends, and Pity ; whilft I will advance
Thy Younger Brother to thy loft Eftate,
And fee thee ftarve; nay, more, and loaded with
The Curfes of thy Father———

Pier. Hold, Sir!———
I'le ftrive t' obey you; not becaufe I fear
What Mifery, or Death can do to me;
Nor to avoid the hungry Lyon's Den,
Or Dragons Teeth, juft ready to devour me ;
For know, I plunge into a State more dreadful:
But that I may not be th' unhappy Caufe
Of dragging wrongful Curfes from a Father,
Which rather turn upon his Head that aims,
Than hurt the Bofom of the Innocent.

Enter Diana.

North. See! fhe is coming, brighter than a Goddefs———
I'le leave you, and commit you to her Cure.   [*Ex.* North.

Dian. Yonder's the dear-lov'd Man, whom all muft love,
That loves another too. What fhall I fay ?   [*Afide.*
Spite of my Stars, I dote upon a Perfon,
Who has no Heart, no Eyes that are his own ;
Nor yet one look that ever can be mine.

Pier. Madam! d' you hear the news? My Father tells me,
W'are to be Marry'd.

Dian. So the King will have it.

Pier. The King! What would the Tyrant be a God ?

G   To

To take upon him to difpofe of Hearts!
And joyn unequal Souls with one another!
O Beautiful *Diana*! Y'are all Goodnefs,
A ftore of Virtues in as bright a Perfon,
As Heav'n e're treafur'd in a Form Divine :
If fo, what can your Eyes behold in me ?
What fee in fuch a wretched thing as I,
To Marry me?

    Dian. How Charming is his Perfon *!*
And much more Charming is his Grief *!* And oh ———
How can fhe e're receive a Wound more deadly,   [*Afide.*
Than I, tormented with the double Dart
Of Love and Pity—Some kind Deity
Affift me now, left I fhould fhew I love him,
And teach my Tongue how to bely my Heart.

    Pier. You feem to ftudy for fo plain an Anfwer.
Come tell me ftreight my faults, and what you think ;
For here I ftand, the Mark of Truth to aim at.
What is there, in this miferable Shape,
To look on without Scorn ?

    Dian. Now kind, Heav'n,
Lend me the Cunning now of all my Sex !   [*Afide.*
I like you juft as well as you like me ;   [*To* Piercy.
Our Perfons might, for all you faid of mine,
Be mended both, and both receive Additions :
And for your Nature, I'le be plain, and tell you,
I could have wifh'd a Man of better humour ;
But 'tis no matter, fince w'are both fo bad,
We are the fitter then for one another.
Juft Gods ! what miferable Things we are!   [*Afide.*
Oh ! when fhall we attain that bleft abode,
Where we may never fear to fpeak aloud,
What's Juft, and is no Sin ?

    Pier. What, do you hate me ?
Then y'are happier one Degree than I ;
For fhould you love me. you are truly wretched.

    Dian. Indeed he little thinks I am that Wretch.   [*Afide.*
Tell me wherefore ?   *To* Piercy.

    Pier. Becaufe the Cruel God
Has rob'd me of my whole Eftate of Love,

                                  And

And left me naked, defolate, and poor;
Not worth one Sigh, nor Wifh, if that could pay
The Debt I owe: Nay, fhould you come a begging,
Cold, and half ftarv'd, for Succour to my door,
You would not find, in all this rifled Cottage,
One Spark, one Charitable Spark, to warm you.
 Dian. Hear, Heav'n! hear, Cruel One! who-e're thou art
He loves, tho I am flighted, fcorn'd, nay hated, [*Afide.*
Wou'd thou hadft my Kind Eyes, my Breaft, my Soul,
Would all my Vital Blood were Balm to Cure him.
Yet will our Cruel Parents have us Marry'd: [*To* Piercy.
Then, fince we muft, how know we but our Bodies,
And yet more Carelefs and Defpairing Souls,
In time may grow to fuch Indifference,
As quite forgetting of what Sex we are,
We may like faithful and condoling Friends,
If not like Lovers, live together.
 Pier. Ay;
And when y'are fad, I'le Kifs you like a Brother;
And if you figh, or chance to fhed a Tear,
I will weep too, and ask you why you grieve;
And you fhall do the like to me, and ftreight
Embrace me like a Sifter, ftill remembring
The Subject of our juft Complaints fhall be,
You that y'are Marry'd———
 Dian. You for Marrying me.
 Pier. O rarely thought! 'twill be the only Means
To make us happy both againft our Wills;
We'll moan, we'll figh, we'll weep; we'll all but love——
Inftead of loving, pity one another.
 Dian. And who can tell but Pity may at laft,
By gentle, foft Degrees, grow up to Love.
 Pier. Come, let's away then, fince they'll have it fo;
Meet thefe glad Rites to all Mankind but us,
Where the malicious Charm fhall join our Curfes,
And not our Perfons, but our Woes together:
Then turn us loofe, like two Condemn'd, lone Wretches;
Banifht from Earth, no Creature but our felves,
In an old Bark on wide and Defart Seas,
In Storms by Night and Day, unfeen by all,
Unpity'd,

Unpity'd toft, not one dear Morfel with us
To eafe our Hunger, nor one drop of Drink
To quench our raging Thirft, and which is worfe,
Without one jot of Rigging, Sail, or Steer to guide us.

    Dian. Forgive me, Heav'n! Forgive me all my Sex,   [*Afide.*
That ever lov'd, or e're was fcorn'd like me!
Tho 'tis my Fate for ever to be hated,
Tho we are doom'd to dwell, like wandring Wretches,
In worfe than what his worft of Sorrow paints ;
Yet I muft love him, and refolve to Marry him ;
And now I challenge all the wondring World,
And more admiring Angels, if they can,
To find who moft is to be pity'd, He
Or I—Quick, let us launch then with a Courage,   [*To* Piercy.
Since 'tis our King and Cruel Parents Wills.

    Pier. And give a rare Example to the Marry'd,
Of Conftancy : For that which fevers them,
Poffeffion of their pall'd and loath'd Enjoyments,
Our faithful Woes fhall join our Lives the fafter.

    Dian. And having each of us fo mean a Stock
Of love, I in your Breaft, and you in mine ;
We need not fear that Thieves fhould come to rob us.

    Pier. Nor Jealoufie to part us.

    Dian. Well then, *Piercy :*
When our expected Sentence is perform'd,
Where fhall we take our welcome Banifhment ?

    Pier. To the World's End ! Far from all fruitful Grounds,
From Corn, and VVine, or any wanton Spring ;
In fome dead Soil, fo barren and fo curft,
Where neither loathfom Weeds, nor Thiftles grow.

    Dian. Or fome deep Cave, where Winds are all fo ftill,
And Beafts fo far remote, that we fhall hear
No Howls, nor Groans, but what we make our felves.

    Pierc. No : on fome dreadful Rock we'll chufe to lye,
Whofe difmal Top feems faften'd to the Skye ;
Thence we can look on all the World below,
So full of Vanity, fo full of Woe !
And fometimes on the Wrack-devouring Seas,
The Emblem of our prefent Miferies.:

                                      Sigh

Sigh for the Creatures, think the Storms we fee
Our Cruel Parents, and the Wretches We.

    Dian. Or wafte our Days in wandring to and fro,
And make our Lives one Harmony of Woe.

    Pier. 'Till Heav'n fhall rain down pity on us——

    Dia. No.
We'll not be pity'd. Pity's half a Cure ;
That will bring Comfort, which we'll ne're endure.

    Pier. O my *Virago* Partner.

    Dian. Nay, I dare you.

    Pier. Then here we'll take an Oath, and with this Kifs.
Let's ftrike a League with Woe, adieu to Blifs!
And now I challenge the All-feeing Sun,
From his proud Profpect, his high Seat at Noon;
'Mongft all the Wonders of the World, to fpy
A Couple half fo kind as thee and I;
Or all the Matches that e're Love decreed,
If ever Man and Wife fo well agree'd.
Love oft-times flies from Mifery and Pain ;
But we refolve the clofer to remain.
What though we Wed in Hatred, we may mend;
We but begin where others furely end;
And each of you that Marry firft for love,
VVe are but fooner, what at laft you'll prove.   *[Ex. Ambo.*

The End of the Third Act

A.C.T.

ACT IV. SCENE I.

Enter Blunt *with Letters,* Rochford.

Blunt. MY Lord, you act the cunning Lover well,
       Paint a rare Paſſion under all Diſguiſes;
Yet oh! I wiſh this Art had not been learnt,
But Nature in you, and true Love the Teacher;
Yet I will prize and hoard your Letters ſafe,
As I would fragrant Flowers within my Boſom.
   Roch. O my prodigious and exalted Soul,
And my more precions Stars! I bleſs you all.
Is there a Man 'mongſt all your Favourites,
So rich, ſo happy, and ſo lov'd as I!
Methinks, for my dear *Anna Bullen's* ſake,
If poſſible, I love you better now,
Since I dare call you by the Name of Siſter.
   Blunt. And I much more now I can call you Brother.
   Roch. O my too weighty Joys! Immortal State!
And more Immortal Love!
   Blunt. No more: I'le chide you.
This is too great, too violent to laſt———
Hold! give your Paſſion Breath, leave ſome for next,
And love not all your VViſhes out at once———
Where is the Queen?
   Roch. I left her diſcontent.
   Blunt. Why, where is *Piercy?* Has ſhe ſeen him yet?
   Roch. Seen him ſhe has: but would not ſpeak to him.
   Blunt. Not ſpeak to him! Oh Cruel, moſt Inhumane!
Had ſhe but ſeen him in that ſtate as I did,
She would have ſpoke to him, and dy'd for him.
   Roch. Alas! Her Cruelty drew Pity from
Her Eyes and Mine.
   Blunt. Would ſhe not ſpeak t' him then!
   Roch. No; not a word: but quite o're-came her Pity,
And went away reſolv'd ne're more to ſee him.
   Blunt. The Reaſon.

                                        Roch.

Roch. She'd not tell————But I moſt doubt
Her ſcrupulous Virtue is the Cauſe.
 Blunt. Impoſſible!
Virtue can never lodge with Cruelty.
What ſtain were it to th' whiteſt Innocence?
What Crime in the ſevereſt Virtue once,
In her Condition, but to hear him ſpeak?
Come! ſhe muſt ſee him————
 Roch. Would my Life, and Fortune,
Nay, all my Rights of Love, and Hopes in thee,
Could purchaſe her Conſent to ſeem him once,
Pardon the Sallies of moſt mighty Friendſhip,
So well I wiſh him, I would hazard all.
 Blunt. Go tell, as from your ſelf, the ſad condition
Her horrid Cruelty has brought him to.
Within this hour he enter'd my Apartment,
Not like the Great, the Brave, and Charming *Piercy,*
Whoſe Perſon none cou'd ſee without adoring:
But like a dreadful Ghoſt, or horrid Shadow,
Far worſe than what dead, melancholly Midnight,
To frighted Man, e're painted in a Dream;
The Evil Genius of his Family
Ne're look'd ſo mad, nor threaten'd half the Woe,
As he did to himſelf.
 Roch. Unhappy *Piercy.*
 Blunt. At firſt his ſight was pointed to the Earth,
Then with a Groan, charg'd with a Volley of Sighs,
He lifted up his fatal Eyes on me, which I
Could ſcarce behold with mine, they were ſo full
Of pitying Tears————
Then ran into ſuch bitter, ſad Complaints
Againſt our Sexes loath'd Inconſtancy,
That I was forc'd to chide him————
 Roch. Oh, no more!
It wakes my drowſie Conſcience from its reſt,
And ſtabs it with a Guilt.
 Blunt. But then at laſt
From Railings into Bleſſings ſtreight he fell,
And on his Knees beſeech'd me that I'd plead,
And beg the Queen, but once to ſee her *Piercy;*

Which

Which I, rack'd with Compaffion, promis'd him.
Alas! I fear more than I can perform:
This faid, I rife, and *Piercy* follow'd me;
Therefore I charge you, by the Power of Friendfhip,
By *Piercy*'s Woes, and all the Love you owe
To me! go and prevail that he may fee her:
He faid that you had vow'd to bring't to pafs.

   Roch. I'le do it inftantly; and if fhe will not,
I'le bear her Body in thefe Arms by Force;
Her mind, I'm fure, is willing to be with him.

   Blunt. She's coming ftreight this way; go quickly you,
(The miferable Wretch is yet without,)
And give him notice, now's the time to fpeak t'her,
Then ftreight return to hold her in Difcourfe
Till *Piercy* comes.

   Roch. So kind and pitiful!
May all thy Cruel Sex be bleft for thee.   [*Ex.* Roch.

   Blunt. So——this has prov'd a lucky Tale, and now
This rare Intelligence goes to my *Woolfey*,
Who'l fend th' Alarm to the watchful King,
Streight to furprize him with his Wife, like *Jafon*,
Juft ftealing of his Golden Fleece away——
She comes, fhe comes, this Player-Queen; but know,
This is the laft proud Act of all thy fhow;
This is a Bait, kind Stars, if you'l not frown,
With which I'le take Revenge, or catch a Crown:
And when fh' has got her Heav'n, and I my Aim;
Who then dares tell me that I was to blame!
For who contemns a profp'rous Wickednefs,
Or thinks that ill, that's Sainted with Succefs.   [*Ex.* Blunt.

Enter Queen *with a Letter.*

   Queen. What fhall I do! where teach my trembling Feet
Their way! was ever Virtue ftorm'd like mine!
Within, without, I am haunted all alike;
Without tormented with a jealous King,
Within, my Fears fuggeft a thoufand Plagues,
Bid me remember injur'd *Piercy*'s Wrongs,
And brand me with the Name of Cruel to him;

                      Then

Then on a fudden a more dreadful thought
Upbraids me with a Guilt;
And tells me, that kind Pity is a Sin.
Witnefs, and blame not me, y'Immortal Powers!
When you expofe two diff'rent Paths, one Good,
The other bad, and tell not which to take:
If to obey you is my Aim, juft Heav'n!
'Tis not my fault if I fhou'd chufe the wrong.

Enter Rochford.

Roch. Sifter! moft Royal, Merciful, and Fair,
And beft belov'd of Heav'n, and all Mankind,
Let your dear Brother make it his Requeft,
Thus on his Knees, as Deities are Charm'd,
That you would hear th' unhappy *Piercy* fpeak,
This once, and but this once——*Piercy*'s without;
Shall my beft Friend take but his laft Farewell?
Grant it, or never more let *Rochford* fee you.
Queen. Oh Brother! plead no more, 'tis all in vain;
Do not betray thy Sifter to a Guilt,
And ftain the Cryftal Virtue of a Soul,
Which ftill fhe holds far dearer than a Crown;
Seek not, by Vile Enchantments, to deftroy
That Innocence which yet is all my Force,
All the Defence poor *Bullen* has againft
A jealous Husband, Cruel Foes, and worfe,
Againft the Malice of Inveterate Hell.
Roch. What Danger can there be? what Guilt in you?
To hear the Wretched and the Injur'd pray?
Come; for you will, you fhall, you muft now hear him.
Queen. No more! no more. There's yet a fubtler Orator
Than you, or Pity, pleads for *Piercy* here,
Here in my firm couragious Soul, and ftronger
Than Father, Mother, or ten thoufand Brothers,
Yet I can that deny.
Roch. What fhall I tell him?
Queen. Tell him, we are undone; I muft not fee him;
And what's far worfe, the King is jealous; tell him
I love him——Tell him what is falfe, I hate him;

H   Say

Say any thing; but let me not behold him;
For oh! my Weakneſs he ſo fierce aſſaults,
'Twill ſpoil——'Twill wrack my Conduct——See, he comes.

Enter Piercy.

Moſt Cruel Piercy !——Cruel Brother rather——
Help—Take, and bear me ſwiftly from the Danger.
   Roch. Caſt but one Look, and you muſt needs relent.
   Queen. What ſhall I do? which Paſſage ſhall I chuſe? [*Aſide.*
Arm me, kind Heav'n! againſt my Foe of Pity.
   Pier. Still, ſtill ſhe turns, and hides her treach'rous Eyes—
Is't poſſible that ſhe can feel Remorſe?
Or Pity after all? O no; ſhe loves too well
The fatal Cauſe that purchas'd all this Pomp —
Stay, *Anna Bullen!* Stay; my Queen—Perhaps
It is expected I ſhould call you Queen:
Behold your Hatred——
   Queen. Fly, good *Piercy,* fly:
There's Nets preparing for your life and mine——
There's nought but Snares and Quick-ſands where we tread,
Unfathom'd Pits hid under painted Grounds
Where vaſt Deſtruction watches to devour us:
Farewell——
   Pier. Hear me but firſt, and ſhew thy Face,
Thy falſe, diſſembling Beauties——
Many when wrackt have been by Dolphins born,
And ſafely landed on the welcome Shore:
And in the Foreſts, nay, the Monſters Dens,
The Paſſenger, half ſtarv'd for want of Food,
Has by the Lyons oft been ſpar'd and fed:
But Cruel *Bullen,* Cruel Beauty kills
All whom it Fetters, moſt on whom it Smiles.
Nor can the Elements, nor gentler Brutes,
Teach Woman to be pitiful or good.
   Queen. Now, now juſt Heav'n! y'are ſhowring all your Plagues,
At once upon my Head, and I will bear 'em;
Bear 'em like one of you, and bleſs the Weight;
Hear my ſelf falſe upbraided, call'd moſt perjur'd,
Deceitful, and the Monſter of my Sex;
Ev'n I, (who, you Revengeful Powers above   Know,)

Know,) love this Cruel Chider to a Fault!
Ah *Piercy, Piercy*——Fly ; for life begone ;
Each Minute that you ſtay brings Death to both.

Pier. Ah, hold! If not for Love, for Pity ſtay.
And if no juſt Complaint can pierce your hearing,
Then Bleſſings ſhall: Ten thouſand Bleſſings on you,
If you will hear the Curſt of Mankind ſpeak.

Roch. Now, Siſter, heard you that! By Heav'n it melts me.
Sure I'm turn'd all the Woman, you the Man.

Queen. Give me your hand, kind Brother, and ſupport me ;
Help, for I ſtagger with the treble Weight
Of Grief, Deſpair, and Pity!
My Senſes all are charm'd, and Feet faſt ty'd
To this Inchanted Floor——Quick, or I'm loſt.

Pier. Yet turn ; if there's one jot of Pity in you ;
If *Piercy* e're was worth one Thought, I charge you,
By the lov'd Name of *Anna Bullen,* ſtay——
What then, will nothing move? O inexorable!
No not a Look! not *Piercy* worth one Look!
Yet, *Rochford,* hold! Canſt thou too be ſo Cruel!
Fell and obdurate both!
Is there no hope? but will you; will you then
Begone?

Queen. Fly, Brother, e're it be too late,
For ſhou'd I liſten but a Moment more,
The ſtrength of *Hercules* were not enough
To draw me hence, ſo unruly is my Body,
And my unwilling Soul ſo loth to part.

Pier. Then with my Knees, thus faſtning to the ground

             [Piercy *kneels upon her Robe.*

Your Robe, and thus with my extended Arms
I'le force and charm you, 'till y'have heard my laſt
Complaint: And then forbear to pity if you can.

Queen. Why doſt thou hold?—— Why do I hold my ſelf?

Pier. Ten thouſand Curſes light upon her Soul
In Hell; and worſe, what mine on Earth endures,
That firſt taught Woman Falſehood——
If for a Crown ſhe's falſe! Oh may that Crown
Sit loathſom on her Forehead as her Crimes,
May Adders neſt within th' Ambitious Round,

And into Stings the fatal Ermins turn.
When dead, may all the Miseries she feels
Be through the World recorded as a Mark
For faithful Lovers to beware, and ne're
Be nam'd without a Curse.

    Queen. Ah Cruel *Piercy!*

    Pier. But for my Queen, let Heav'n and Angels guard her;
Her I except from any bitter Fate:
Let *Anna Bullen's* Breast be ne're disturb'd,
Nor Soul upbraided with the Wrongs of *Piercy*:
And oh, kind Heav'n! if there be any Sorrow
(As sure none e're can be) ordain'd for her,
False as she is, I beg that it may fall
Only on wretched *Piercy's* Head——May Hers
Be all the Pleasure still, and mine the Pain.

    Queen. O Gods! obdurate Heav'ns! Cruel Honour! [*Aside.*
And yet more Cruel Vertue, hear and see!

    Pier. And when I shall for ever be recluse,
As now I go to part with all Mankind,
'Twill be my Joy, sometimes to think of you,
And make me live, perhaps, one Day the longer,
When in my Melancholy Cell, I hear
That the Crown flourishes on *Bullen's* Head.

    Queen. Ha! I'm or'ewhelm'd, the Sluces all are broke, [*Aside.*
And Pity, like a Torrent, pours me down;
Now I am drowning, all within's a Deluge;
Wisdom nor Strength can stem the Tide no more,
And Nature in my Sex ne're felt the like ——
Help *Rochford*, e're I'm rooted to this Earth.
Away, away! the least word more undoes me.

    Pier. Yet turn one Look upon me, e're you go.

    Queen. There, take it, with my life, perhaps the purchase—
Take that too, *Piercy*, thou hast been betray'd. [*Gives him a*
Learn there th'unhappy *Bullen's* Fate----Farewell.   *Letter.*

    Pier. Yet stay---the Soul ne're parted with such pangs,
From the pale Body, as you fly from me.

    Queen. Piercy adieu----I can----I will----I must
No more.   [*Ex.*Qu. *and* Roch.

    Pier. What, never see you more! She's gone,
She's gone, more lov'd and beautiful than ever:

And

And now methought, juſt as ſhe parted from me,
She ſhot a Look quite through my gory Heart,
And left it Gaſping, Dying, and Deſpairing ———
What's here, a Letter! and the Character
That I ſo oft have been acquainted with?
If theſe Eternal Kiſſes give me leave,
I'le break it open with as great a Joy,
As I had leap'd into our Marriage-Bed,
And rifled all the Sweets and Pleaſures there——
What's this I read!

Reads.

> By *Wicked* Woolſey, Harry, *and our Parents*
> *I was betray'd, and forc'd to Wed the King :*
> *Who intercepted all thy Letters, Swearing*
> *With Sacramental Oaths, that thou wert falſe,*
> *And Marry'd Firſt——*Piercy *adieu, and Credit me,*
> *And that I lov'd thee better than my Life.*
> *Burn this raſh Paper, leſt the Fiends diſcloſe it.*
> B V L L E N.

She's Innocent! Oh! you Immortal Powers!
She's Innocent! And then ſhe loves me ſtill.
Sound, found my Joy, till my Exalted Soul
Is wound up to th' extreameſt pitch of Bliſs:
Let *Piercy* never after this be ſad———
Yet hold——What dawn of Comfort can'ſt thou ſpy
In this——Oh none——This Gloworm-Spark,
This Glimps of Hope is vaniſht, and I'm left
In deeper Darkneſs, Horrour and Deſpair,
Than e're I was before——
Oh *Anna Bullen*! Curſt in being true!
And I more Curſt in knowing it too late.

Re-enter Queen *and* Rochford.

Ha! ſhe returns! The mourning Angel comes
Again! Sure Heav'n's in Love with both our Miſeries,
They look with ſuch a Pomp and Train in me;

And

And are ſo beautiful in her!

Queen. Well, Brother,
And thou far ſtronger and Immortal Pity,
And more Immortal Love, y' have brought me back——
Ye have. What! what will you do with me now?

Roch. Could any thing on Earth! Tyger, or Panther,
Much leſs a Creature form'd by Heav'n like It:
Could you, I ſay, refrain at ſuch an Object!
At the laſt Words of the unhappy Wretch,
And not forbear to balm him o're in Tears,
Or elſe but hear him ſpeak!

Queen. Now I'm incloſ'd again!
The Combat now grows fierce and ſtrong, and oh!
How weak an Armour Reſolution is,
Againſt our Paſſions, or the Man belov'd:
Virtue and Honour, hence be proud no more,
Nor brag of your Dominion o're Mankind;
Leſt Love, moſt fatal Love, too ſoon ſhould tell you,
And make you feel, h' has mightier Chains than you——
See where he is——Look Heav'n with tender Eyes;
Give Council to my juſt deſpairing Soul,
And tell me, Pity is no Sin——Ah *Piercy!*

Pier. My Charming Queen! my *Anna Bullen* once!
Am I ſo Bleſt, and yet ſo wretched too,
As what is written here contains; and tell me!
May I believe that you can love me ſtill?

Queen. Oh *Piercy! Piercy!* urge me not to tell you
What Heav'ns Auſterity will not permit,
Nor force me to declare——
What the *Eternal* Sees already written
In too broad Characters within my Breaſt;
How large, how deep thy Story's graven here,
And what I dare not, never muſt unfold——.
Oh! I have ſaid too much.

Pier. What! ſaid too much!
Can you repent of one kind thought of *Piercy?*
And ſpitefully call back your tender Mercy!
Nay, worſe; Can you behold the almoſt Naked,
And ſtarv'd beſeeching Wretch, and ſtrive to pull
The totter'd Remnants from his quivering Joints,

And

And dafh the Pitcher from the greedy Lips
Of one juft ready to expire with Thirft?
Oh Cruel Queen! For *Anna Bullen* would not,
She would not, would not ufe her *Piercy* thus.

   Queen. Ceafe, ceafe fuch founds——
And turn thy fad, refiftlefs Eyes away;
For if I once behold thofe Tears, and hear
Thy juft Complaints, I can no longer hold,
But break I muft through all the bonds of Virtue.
Nay, ftood the Jealous *Harry* by
With all his Guards of Devils, *Woolfey's, Cardinals*;
In fpight of all, in fpight of more my felf
I muft both fee, hear thee, and fpeak to thee,
And pity thee. Now are you fatisfied?

   Pier. It is enough, bright Daughter of the Sky:
Y' have conquer'd me, my Deity, you have
Here on my Knees, but yet at diftance too,
The Pofture of a Soul in Extacy,
I beg a thoufand Pardons of my Queen.
A Look, a Sigh, or Tear, from *Anna Bullen*,
Is far more worth than all the trifling Wrongs;
Nay, than the Life and very Soul of *Piercy.*

   Queen. Help me juft Heav'n, who fees how I'm befieged,
And what a weak Refiftlefs Wretch I am!
Why d'ye impofe on us fo hard a Task
On poor Mankind, fo feeble and fo frail,
Making us here Comiffioners of Virtue,
Yet put by Drams and Scruples in the Ballance,
To Counter-poife and weigh down Flefh and Blood.
How weaks my Will to draw my Body hence;
And oh! how loath my Eyes are to depart,
But wifh for ever to be faften'd on thee,
And look one Look to vaft Eternity;
Yet we muft part, Ah, *Piercy*! part for ever——

   Pier. Ah fay not fo! muft we fo foon, my Queen!
Is then this Moments Blifs fo Criminal,
That it muft forfeit all my precious Hopes
Of an Affurance once to meet again!

   Queen. My mind now bodes to me, that 'tis our laft:
Yet I muft bid thee go: There is no Joy for us;

The World's a Deluge all to thee and me———
There is no reft, my *Piercy*, in this World,
No Sanctuary to lay the weary Head
Of the undone, th' unpitty'd, and betray'd.
Farewell: There's fomewhat rifes o're my Soul,
And covers it as with a fatal Cloud
Of Horror, Death, and Fear. It cannot be;
The Sting of parting cannot do all this;
Farewell, farewell.

 Pier. Stay; muft we part for ever?
What never! never meet again!

 Queen. Never till we are Clay, and then perhaps,
Neglected as we were in Life, thrown out in Death,
Some Charitable Man may be fo kind,
To give our poor forfaken Bodies Burial,
Laying 'em both together in one Bed
Of Earth.———
Hah! the times come! my Fatal Doom's at Hand!

    Three Drops of Blood falls from her Nofe,
     and ftains her Handkerchief.

Behold, the Heav'ns in Characters of Blood,
In three inevitable Drops,
Have feal'd it, and decreed that it is now!
Ah *Piercy*! fly, and leave me here alone
To ftem this mighty Torrent of my Fate.
Begone, while I have Life to bid thee go:
For now Death ftops my Tongue.——— [*She Swoones.*

 Pier. My Lord———
She Faints——My Life! my *Anna Bullen* ftay;
Or your Commands fhall Fetter me no more;
But break I will through all the Bars of Diftance,
And catch thee thus, thus hold thee in my Armes———
Rochford! Oh help to call her back again.
Hold, ftop thy flight; thou precious Air return!
Far richer than that rare Immaculate Breath,
Which Natures God breath'd in the firft of Mankind!

 Roch. Wake Sifter, wake! behold, no dangers nigh!

 Queen. Ah *Piercy*! Now I wake, with Courage now
To meet my Fate; and fee where it approaches.

            Enter

Enter Cardinal, Northumberland, *and Guards.*

Pier. Ha! *Woolsey*, and my Father with the Guards!
Card. My Lord, e're we discover our Commission,
Pray, let your Son be parted from the Queen,
Left the wrong'd King should see him in his Rage,
And Execute his worst of Fury on him.
  North. Son! tho' you have committed, in the Court,
The greatest Crime, against your Royal Master,
That e're a Subject can be guilty of;
Yet in respect of these Gray Hairs and Tears,
He has been pelas'd to spare your forfeit Life:
Therefore begone: A Minutes stay is fatal————
Guards, force him, if he goes not willingly,
And carry him streight, by Barge, to *Suffolk*-House
Without Reply.
  Pier. Obediently I'le go,
If you will promise me that you have nought
Against the Sacred Person of the Queen,
And will not touch her: For 'tis greater Sacriledge,
Then 'tis to hurt an Angel, cou'd it be,
She is so Innocent, so Chast, and Pure.
Else I'm resolv'd to stand, no Rock so firm!
Fixt like the Center to the Massey Globe.
You should as soon remove strong *Hercules*,
With his Hands grasping both the Poles of Heaven,
As force me from this Footing, where I stand,
And see the Queen but threatned, or in danger.
  Card. My Lord, on both our Honours, the Queens Person
Shall be Inviolate and Sacred always;
Nor know we ought against her—but the King
Is coming streight to visit her, as kindly
As he was wont: Therefore you must begone——
We have no other Reason, but your safety.
  Pier. I fear! for ah what Truth can come from thee?
Thou speak'st but at the Second Hand from Hell——
Kind Sir, May I believe what *Woolsey* says?
  Card. Confirm it, good my Lord, or you'l delay.
  North. 'Tis true, what the great Cardinal has told you.

I

Queen. Go, *Piercy*; and miſtruſt not more than I;
Begone, if I have Power left to Command;
Leave me to Innocence, and Heav'n that will not
Permit a Soul that never did any ill,
To fear it.

    Pier. Then I'le go———But oh Juſt Heav'n !
And all you Angels, Cherubins, and Thrones :
All you bright Guards to the moſt High Imperial,
You kindeſt, gentleſt, mildeſt Planets,
You leſſer Stars, you fair Innumerable,
And all you bright Inhabitants above,
Protect the Sacred Perſon of the Queen ;
And ſhed your balefull'ſt Venom on their Heads,
That think to ſtain a Whiteneſs like your ſelves.
Farewell———
                          [*Ex.* Piercy.

    Queen. Farewell*!*
    Card. John Viſcount *Rochford,* by the King's Command,
W' Arreſt you here, of Capital, High Treaſon.
    Queen. Hear Heav'n! my Brother faln into the Snare !
    Card. And 'tis his Pleaſure, that you ſtreight be ſent
Cloſe Priſoner to the *Tower,* with the Lord *Norris,*
Who is ſuſpected with you to be Guilty
Of the ſame hainous Crime. Guards! Seize his Perſon.
    Roch. Baſe Villain! Traytor! *Woolſey*! Say, for what?
    Queen. No matter. Let a Woman teach thee Courage:
Ne're ask for what, ſince 'tis his wiſe Decree
Above who gave us with a liberal Hand,
And ſate us on the higheſt Spoke of Greatneſs,
No longer than he pleaſ'd to call us down———
Well, Whoſe turn's next? Come, dart your worſt, my Lords,
And meet a temper'd Breaſt, that knows to bear.
By my bright Hopes, y' are more afraid than I ;
I did expect you would begin with me !
    Card. Moſt Royal Madam, Oh! I wiſh the King
Had choſen ſome leſs unwilling than our ſelves,
To Execute this moſt deteſted Office.
In Witneſs of it, on our Knees, with Tears
                          [*Kneels.*
And Sorrow, we our ſad Commiſſion tell:
It is the Kings moſt fatal Pleaſure too,
That you be ſent a Priſoner to the *Tower,*

                                  And

And thence, immediately to both your Tryals.   [*Rises.*

Roch. Tryal! oh her wrong'd Innocence! for what?

Queen. No more, Dear Brother; let us both submit,
And give Heav'n Thanks, and our most Gracious King;
For I'm not so presumptuous of my Virtue;
But think, Dear *Rochford*, that both you and I
Have once committed, in our erring Lives,
Something, for which we justly merit Death.
Though not, perhaps, the Thing we are accused of.

Enter the King *in a Fury, with Letters in his Hand.   Attendants and Guards.*

Card. The King is here!

Queen. Then he is Merciful.

King. Where is this Woman! this most abhorr'd of Wives!
This Scandal to her Sex, my Crown and Life!
What by your Minion? oh good Natur'd Husband!
Down on your Knees, and thank me for the favour——
See——here are Letters faln into my Hands,
Where your dear Brother says he has enjoy'd you.
                [*Gives the Letters to the* Queen
Oh thou more Damn'd, and more Insatiate far,
Than *Messalina.*   She was Chast, to thee.
Her, half the Men and Slaves of *Rome*,
Could satisfy; but thou, not all Mankind,
With Husband, Brother, Kindred in the Number. [*She gives*

Queen. Oh Heav'nly Pow'rs! oh Guard of Innocence! ['*em* Roch.
What do I see and hear! O Sacred Sir!
You took me to your Royal Bed, a Hand-maid,
The most unworthy of the mighty Favour;
Oh throw me into Dungeons streight, or take
Away my Life, that ne're offended you:
Take all, in Recompence, from *Anna Bullen!*
'Tis yours; But do not Rob me of my Fame,
Nor stain my Virtue with so foul a Guilt.

Roch. What's here? my Amorous Letters sent to *Blunt*!
Has she betray'd me!

King. I will hear no more——   [*To the Queen.*

Roch. Ah Royal Sir, thefe Letters I confefs——

King. Damn thy hot Luftful Breath; thy Poyfonous Tongue!
Here, take 'em hence, to Tortures, Racks, to Death.

Queen. O Sir! I am prepar'd for any Death;
For worfe than Death, a thoufand, thoufand Torments;
And if you think 'em all not pain enough,
Here, take Advice of *Woolfey*; Hee'l inftruct you;
Tell you, how you may plague this hated Body;
But do not think that I'm fo loath'd a Creature.

King. Quick; Take away thy Hands, or I will force thee——

Queen. You fhall not, cannot, till I've Sworn the Truth:
For, by th' unfpotted Babe within the Womb,
That yet lies wrapt in Innocence, unborn;
By injur'd Truth, by Souls of Martyr'd Saints,
By you, my Lord, my Husband, and my King!
And by the King of Kings, the King of Heav'n,
I'm wrong'd! Ah Royal, gracious Sir, I'm wrong'd.

King. Unhand me; or I'le fpurn thee from thy hold——
Seize, feize on *Piercy*—By my Life, who begs   [*To the Guards.*
In his Behalf's a Traytor, worfe than he——   [*To* North. *who*
Here is another Letter too, it is from *Norris*,   *kneels.*
Who much Commends your darling, fecret Beauties,
And fweetnefs of your Lips; Yet you are wrong'd!——
Here's Notes of your Mufician too, that Charm'd you.
Eternal Hell! where's fuch another Monfter?
I have more Horns than any Forreft yields,
Than *Finsbury*, or all the City Mufters
Upon a Training, or a Lord Mayors-Day.
Rife! and Begon, thou Fiend, thou Sorcerefs;
Thy Power, thy Charms, like Witch-craft, all have left thee,
Go you inceftuous Twins, make hafte and mingle
Your foul, Adulterate Blood in Death together——
Oh, they're too long afunder. Why, doft Weep!
Go to thy Death, and what's a greater pain,
May Heav'n, like me, fee all thofe Tears in vain.

[*Ex.* King, *Attendants*

Roch. Ah Sifter! what dire Fiends muft punifh *Rochford*:
What will become of me, the Caufe of all?

Queen. Fear not. Heav'n knows thy Innocence, and mine!
What tho' we fuffer here a little fhame!

Th

'Tis to reward our Souls above, and with
Immortal Reſtitution Crown 'em there———
We two liv'd in one Mother's ſpotleſs Womb ;
And then we ſcarce had purer Thoughts than now!
And ſhortly we ſhall meet together in
One Grave.

    Roch. O ſay not ſo: Death dare not be ſo Cruel.

    Queen. Ceaſe Brother, ceaſe; ſay not a word in anſwer;
But lead me, like a Valiant Man, to Chains.
Come, let's prepare———But firſt my Pomp adieu !

                         [Kneels, and lays down her Crown.
From Heav'n I did my Crown and Life receive,
And back to Heav'n both Crown and Life I'le give;
And thus, in humble poſture, lay it down
With greater Joy than firſt I put it on.   *[Riſes.*
And now I tread more light, and ſee from far
A Beamy Crown, each Diamond a Star.
But oh, you Royal Martyrs! ceaſe a while
Your Crying Blood, that elſe muſt curſe this Iſle;
Of the *Imperial* ask it with my Pray'r;
For you are ſtill the neareſt Angels there:
Then *Richard, Edwards, Henry,* all make room,
The firſt of ſlaughter'd *Engliſh* Queens I come;
Let me amongſt your glorious, happy Train,
Free from this hated World, and Traitors Reign.   *[Ex. Ambo.*

The End of the Fourth Act.

ACT

ACT V. SCENE I.

Enter Cardinal *and* Blunt *feverally.*

Card. Luckieſt of Omens! do I meet my *Juno!*
My Fair, Illuſtrious Partner in Revenge *!*
Come, tell the News that your glad Eyes proclaim:
Speak, by thy Looks, I know it muſt be well.
Is ſhe Condemn'd *?* Shall *Rome* be Abſolute *?*
Shall *Woolſey* Reign, and ſhall my *Blunt* be Queen *?*
   Blunt. 'Tis as thou ſay'ſt, moſt mighty of thy Function;
Greateſt that e're adorn'd this Robe, it is.
Theſe Eyes ſaw the bright *Engliſh* Sun Eclips'd,
And what is more, Eclips'd by Thee and Me,
Caſt by her aweful Judges from her Height,
Guilty and ſham'd, as *Lucifer* from Heav'n,
And forc'd to beg it, as the mildeſt Sentence,
To loſe her Head.
   Card. Then there's an end of *Bullen.*
   Blunt. And what to ſee, gave me the greater Joy;
Thoſe Letters counterfeited by the Fool
Her Brother, were the ſtrongeſt Proofs againſt her;
So the ſame Papers which by your Advice
I got convey'd into her Cabinet,
Were the ſubſtantiall'ſt Circumſtances found
For which ſhe dies.
   Card. O Juſt and Sacred Rage,
Revenge! Thou greateſt Deity on Earth *!*
And Woman's Wit the greateſt of thy Council.
   Blunt. We ought to veil before your Prieſtly Robe;
My Crown of Wit ſhall ne're ſtand Candidate
With yours; and yet I dare be bold to ſay,
This I, and Malice would have done alone,
Without the mighty Aid of *Woolſey's* Brain.
   Card. Then nothing's to be done by Fate, nor *Woolſey,*
But take the vanquiſht Crown from *Bullen's* Head,
And place it ſuddenly on yours.

Blunt.

Blunt. For which,
My gracious *Woolfey,* I will fo reward you.

Enter to them Piercy.

Pier. Blackneſs Eternal cover all the World *!*
Infernal Darkneſs, ſuch as *Ægypt* felt,
When the Great Patriarch curs'd the fatted Land,
And with a Word extinguiſht all the light.
    Blunt. See, *Piercy*'s here! more mad than we are joyful:
Does't not make young the Blood about thy heart,
T' ſee that our Revenge not fingly hits,
But, like a Chain-ſhot carries all before it?
    Card. Let us avoid him——you intend to ſee
The Queen receive her Death: But I, to hide
The Pleaſure that perhaps the fight would give me,
Will paſs this Day at *Eſher,* like a Mourner.
    Pier. Behold, the Sun ſhines ſtill; inſtead of Darkneſs,
Yon Azure Blue's unſpeckled with a Cloud;
The Face of Heav'n ſmiles on her as a Bride,
The Day, the Sun ſits mounted on his Chariot,
And darts his ſpightful Beams in ſcorn of Pity;
'Bates not a jot of the Illuſtrious Pomp,
He ſhould have furniſh'd on her Wedding-Day:
Heav'n looks like Heav'n ſtill, Nature as 'twas,
Men, Beaſts, and Devils; every thing that lives,
Conſpires, as pleas'd at *Anna Bullen*'s Fall.
Behold, juſt Powers! the Curſes of the Land *!*
Stay you Amphibious Monſters, Prieſt, and Devil ! [*To the Card,*
And Strumpet, if it can be, worſe than both !   *and Blunt.*
You far more dreadful Pair than thoſe that firſt
Betray'd poor eaſie Man, and all Mankind :
Thou fatal Woman Thou *!* and Serpent Thou *!*
By whoſe ſole Malice (oh that Heav'n ſhould let it *!*)
A greater Innocence this Day is fallen,
Than ever bleſt the Walks of Paradiſe.
    Card. My Lord, I ſhall acquaint the King with this,
And thoſe juſt Lords the Judges of her Cauſe,
Whom your baſe Malice wrongs——But I'm above it——
Farewell.   [*Ex.* Card. *and* Blunt.
                            Pier.

Pier. Bold Traytors! Hell-hounds! hear me firft;
Stay you infectious Dragons; do you flye!
Does *Anna Bullen*'s Chaftity and Virtue,
Writ in this Angry Fore-head, make you ftart————[*Exeunt.*

Enter Diana *to him.*

What, the fair, wrong'd *Diana*'s Face in Tears!
Can *Anna Bullen*'s Miferies Attract
The nobleft of Compaffion, Pity from
A Rivals Breaft! thou Wonder of thy Sex!
How far more Wretched mak'ft thou *Piercy* ftill,
When I behold how much thou doft deferve,
And I, fo very little have to pay!
    Dian. What Rocky-heart could have refrain'd from Pity,
To fee the Sight that I did! any thing,
But Man, moft Cruel Mankind, would have griev'd;
Tygers and Panthers would have wept to fee her;
And her bafe Judges, had they not been Men,
Would have bemoan'd her like departing Babes.
    Pier. Is *Rochford* too Condemn'd?
    Dian. Alas! he is.
Rochford and *Norris* both, receiv'd their Sentence,
And both behav'd themfelves like Gallant Men———
But for the Queen! Ah *Piercy*, fuch bright Courage,
No thought can Dictate, nor no Tongue Relate,
When fhe was tax'd with that unnatural Crime,
Adultery with her Brother; ('Tis a Sin
That e're it fhould be nam'd.) At firft fhe ftarted,
And foon an Innocent, not Guilty, Red
Adorn'd her Face, and Sainted it with Tears;
But ftreight conceiving it a Fault, fhe Smil'd,
Wip'd off the Drops, and chid the Blufh away.
    Pier. When I am Dead, may my fad Tale be bleft,
And have no other Tongue, but thine, to tell it.
    Dian. Then with the meeknefs of a Saint fhe ftood;
With fuch amazing Oratory dazled,
And like the Sun, darted quite through her Judges,
And fham'd their Guilt, that none durft look upon her:
But oh! what's deftin'd in the blackeft Pit

Of

Of Hell; what Innocence can n'ere withſtand.
What e're ſhe ſaid, that Angels cou'd not finer,
And ſhew'd a Soul, no Cryſtal nigh ſo clear;
Tho' all appear'd to be the Plot of Devils;
Yet was ſhe guilty found, and, oh, ſad *Piercy* !
(May all Eyes weep at it, like thine and mine)
Condemn'd to loſe her Head.

Pier. Hell dare not think it.

Dian. The Cruel Duke of *Norfolk*, her Relation,
As Steward for the Day, pronounc'd the Sentence.

Pier. And my hard hearted Father too was there.

Dia. My Lord! What ſaid you? your hard hearted Father?
Oh blotted let it be from all Records,
And never be in *Englands* Annals read,
What I'm about to tell you. Her own Father,
The Earl of *Wiltſhire*, ſate amongſt her Judges.

Pier. O Monſter damn'd! than Cruel *Titan* worſe,
That eat up his own Iſſue as he got e'm.

Dia. Behold, the King! All Knees, are bent, all Hands,
All good mens Eyes lift up to Heav'n and him,
To beg the Life of Her that glads the World.

Pier. Make uſe of all thy Womans art to win him;
Let all Petition him that ſhare her Blood,
Matrons, Wives, Virgins, all the charming Sex.

Dia. Do you withdraw. You but incenſe the King——
Iv'e yet a ſoft Experiment to try,
Shall pierce his ſtubborn Nature to the Quick.

Pier. That Angel, th'art inſpir'd with proſper thee. [*Exeunt.*

Enter King *and Attendants.*

King. *Piercy* ! did I not charge he ſhould be ſeiz'd?
                    [*To the Guards who go out to ſeize* Piercy.
Now by the ſacred Crown of *Englands* Monarchs,
Let none entreat me upon pain of Death?   [*To Petitioners.*
What's here? a Liſt of baſe Petitioners,
For *Norris* Life ! Hell and Confuſion ſeize 'em
Have I not like a Rock againſt the Seas,
And Mountain 'gainſt the Winds ſtood thus unſhaken,
Deny'd all *Englands* Prayers, and Tears of Angels?

K   Nay

Nay more, this heart, that pleads with mortal pangs
For my dear *Anna Bullen*'s life? And fhall I
Pardon a Slave before I would my Queen?

Enter Northumberland, *who kneels.*

King. Why doft kneel?
North. I met my Son this moft unlucky moment,
Juft as the Guards were ready to obey,
And Execute your fatal orders on him,
Who in defpair, or rather in obedience,
Making a faint refemblance to refift;
As they were ftriving to put by his Sword,
He on a fudden open'd wide his Arms,
And on his Breaft received a wilful wound.
I kneel with humble Prayer's, that his Difafter
would mitigate your prefent and juft Fury,
And grant my Son his freedom, till his hurt
Is cur'd, which is not mortal.
King. Be it fo.

Enter Diana, *leading in the Young Princefs* Elizabeth, *with Women.*

Dian. Pardon this bold Intrufion in your Prefence.
Your Daughter Sir, this little Princefs here,
Poffeft with Womans Rage, and far above
The little fparkling Reafon of a Child,
Scream'd for her Father; Where's my Father, faid fhe;
And as we brought her to you, ftill fhe cry'd,
Unlefs fhe faw her Father, fhe wou'd die.
King. What wouldft thou have, my little *Betty*, fay?
Child. But will you promife me that you'l not frown,
And cry aloud, Hough? and then indeed I'le tell you.
King. I do. Come, Let me take thee in my Arms——
Child. No: but I'le kneel: for I muft be a Beggar,
And I have learn't, that all who beg of you,
Muft do it kneeling.
North. Prettieft Innocence!
King. well then, what is't my little Pratler, fay?

Child.

Child. I'm told that ftreight my Mother is to die,
Yet I have heard you fay, you lov'd her dearly:
And will you let her die, and me die too?

King. She muft die, Child; There is no harm in death;
Befides the Law has faid it, and She muft.

Child. Muft! is the Law a greater King than you?

King. O yes. But do not cry my pretty *Betty:*
For fhe'l be happier when fhe's dead, and go
To Heaven.

Child. Nay, I'm fure fhee'l go to Heav'n.

King. How art thou fure?

Child. Some body told me fo
Laft night when I was in my fleep.

King. Who was it?

Child. A fine Old man, like my Godfather *Cranmer.*

Card. Ay! there's the Egg that hatcht this Cockatrice.

Child. Pray Father, what's that huge, tall, Bloody man?
I n'ere faw him but once in all my life,
And then he frighted me. He looks for all
The World, juft like the Picture of the Pope.

King. Why, don't you love the Pope?

Child. No indeed don't I,
Nor never will.

King. Ay, but you muft my Dear;
He is a fine old man too, if you faw him.

Card. Go y'are a little Heretick.

Child. A Heretick!
Pray Father, what does that bold Fellow call me?
What's that?

King. Why, that's One that forfakes the right,
And turns to a new, wrong Religion.

Child. Then I'm no Heretick: For I ne're turn'd
In all my life. But you forget your Child.
Dear Father, will you fave my Mother's life?

King. You muft not call me Father: For they fay,
Y'are not my Daughter.

Child. Who's am I then?
Who told you fo? That ugly old, bald Prieft?
He tells untruth. I'm fure you are my Father?

King. How art?

Child. Caufe I love none fo well as you———
But oh you'l never hear me what I have to fay,
As long as He, that Devil there, ftands by
Your Elbow.

King. Ha! what Devil?

Child. That Red Thing there.

King. Oh Child; He is no Devil, he's a Cardinal.

Child. Why does he wear that huge, long Coat then?
Unlefs it be to hide his Cloven Feet.

Card. Sir, all's defign'd by *Cranmer* for the Queen,
Of whom Sh'as learnt this Leffon like a Parot.

King. Take her away. I were a Fool indeed,
If Womens Tears, and Childrens idle Prattle,
Should change my fixt Refolves, and cheat my Juftice———
Away with her.

Child. Oh, but they dare not:
Father, will you not let your *Betty* kifs you?
Why do you let 'em pull me from you fo?
I ne're did anger you:
Pray fave my Mother, Dear King-Father do;
And if you hate her, we will promife both,
That fhe and I will go a great, huge way,
And never fee you more.

King. Unloofe her; hough!
Hence with her ftraight: I will not hear her prate
Another word. Go, y'are a naughty Girl.

Child. Well, I'm refolv'd when I am grown a Woman,
I'le be reveng'd, and cry, Hough, too.

[*Ex.* Diana, Princefs, *Women.*

King. Ha! Spirit !
Mount all the Draw-Bridges, and guard the Gates,
Then bring the Prifoners forth to Execution :
Norris, and *Rochford* firft, and then the Queen :
My Lord *Northumberland,* be it your Task ;
Difpatch my Orders ftraight, and fetch the Traytors———
What's this that gives my Soul a fudden Twitch?
And bids me not proceed. Ha! is't Compaffion!
Shall Pity ever fond the Breaft of *Harry* !
'Tis but a flip of Nature, and I'le on.

                                                    Think

Think on thy Wrongs; the Wrongs her Luſt has done thee,
And ſweep away this loath'd Inceſtuous, Brood,
As Heav'n would drive a Plague from off the Land :
Think thou ſhalt have thy *Seymor* in thy Arms,
Who ſhall reſtore thy loſs with double Charms:
And tho' my *Bullen* ſets this Night, and dies,
Seymor, next Morn, like a new Sun ſhall riſe.
        [*Ex.* King, *Attendants.*
 North. With an unwilling Heart, I take this Office.
And Heav'n, if *Anna Bullen's* Innocent,
Forgive me, ſince it is my King's Command.
My Breaſt is ſad, and tender for her, all;
Tho' *Piercy* ne're can riſe, but by her Fall———

    Enter to him Rochford, Lieutenant, *and Guards.*

 Roch. Wil't not be granted, that I here may ſee
My Siſter e're I dye, to part with her ?
 Lieut. There is my Lord *Northumberland*, he'l tell you.
 Roch. My Lord, y'are come to ſee a wretched Pair
Of *Ormonds* Iſſue leave this fatal World.
Shall we not meet, and take our laſt Farewell ?
 North. *Norris*, my Lord, is now upon the Scaffold.
Then your turn follows; but before that time,
I gueſs the Queen will be prepar'd, and come.
 Roch. Forgive me, Heav'n, my Paſſion, and my Crime,
For Natures choice of a wrong, fatal Object,
Loving too well, what in effect was ill.
O all you ſtrict Idolaters of Beauty !
You fond, ſevere Adorers of that Sex,
Who think that all their Vices cannot Center
In one vile Womans Breaſt; ſee, and repent !
Behold 'em all together
In the Infernal *Blunt*, in Her they're fix'd.
Thus have they all been Curſt, and thus they all
Have been betray'd, that lov'd ſo well as I.

          Enter r

Enter Queen *going to Execution all in White* : Diana,
Women in Mourning; *Guards.*

Queen. Come, where are those must lead me to my Fate?
To a more Glorious, Happy Marriage-Bed,
And my Eternal Coronation Day——
What, *Piercy*'s Father! must he do the Office?
Still I can bear it all, and bear it bravely.

North. Madam! it is the Kings severe Command,
That I attend your Majesty to th' Scaffold.

Queen. Enough, my Lord, you might have spar'd that Title:
Alas! I wish it ever had been spar'd——
I should have been, if Malice had not reign'd,
Your *Piercy*'s Wife, the Scope of my Ambition:
I ne're had then been mounted to a Throne;
Then this unhappy hour had never been.

Roch. Mind this you Rocky World, and mourn in Chaos.
Such Words as these the Heav'ns must weep to hear,
And make yon Marble Roof dissolve in Tears.

Queen. What! do you Weep? to see your Mistress Glory!
That she shall streight wipe off the Stain on Earth
She bears, with an unspotted Fame in Heav'n?
I charge you, by my hopes, and by your hopes,
When you are going where I soon shall go;
By the Illustrious Pomp I long to meet,
The Sacred, Just Rewards of injur'd Truth;
Acquaint this Noble Lord, and all here present,
If e're you saw in all my Nights, or Days,
Or in my looser Hours of Mirth or Humour,
The smallest sign of that most horrid Guilt
That I'm condemn'd for?——Why, are you all dumb?
If you are loth to tell it whilst I live,
Proclaim it when I'm dead, to all the World,
That Heav'n may bar the Gates of Bliss against me,
And throw me to the blackest of Hells Dungeons,
Where all Dissemblers at their Death shall howl.

Wom. Alas! most Gracious Mistress, none can wish
Themselves more Innocent for Death than you.

Queen. What dost thou weep, unhappy Brother too!

Oh

Oh fhew me not fufpected, nor thy felf
So Guilty, by fuch foftnefs——Learn of me!
This Breaft that's petrify'd by conftant Woes!
By all my Wrongs, m' Injuftice, and my Caufe,
Who fees me weep, they fhall be tears of Joy.
Who grieves to leave the World, fhall never come
Where I am going, where all forrow's banifh'd.

Roch. Tho' I am innocent, my Fate is not;
'Tis that has been unjuft to thee and me.

Queen. Tho' 'tis a Common, 'tis a fatal fign,
We weep when we are born: but it was
More ominous, and much more fatal prov'd,
From thefe prophetick Eyes there gufht a fhower,
When *Harry* gave his Faithlefs hand to me;
And on my Coronation day the like,
My bodeing Heart another Tribute rack'd,
Methought there fate a Mountain on my Head,
The Curfes of wrong'd *Katherine* weigh'd me down;
And made my Crown indeed a Maffey Crown.

Roch. Deny me not a little tender Grief,
For every drop of Blood that's to be fhed,
Of that ineftimable Mafs of thine,
My Soul muft rack a thoufand years in Hell.

Queen. Forbear fuch words——You have not injur'd me!
I might as well tax Providence, as you:
For Heav'n, that heard the Perjury of Villains,
Might, if it pleas'd, have chok'd 'em with its Thunder,
Or fent 'em with a Lightning blaft to Hell!
But he has bent their Rage another way,   [*One whifpers* North.
And on their Malice we fhall fafely mount,
As on a Cherubin to Heav'n.

North. My Lord,
You muft prepare; a Meffenger is come,
Who brings the News that *Norris* is beheaded.

Queen. Alas! unhappy *Norris*! art thou dead?
Yet why do I fo much wrong to pity thee?
Thou'rt happier by fome moments now than I.

Roch. Come! lead me to my reft, my reft from wrongs.
Now, *Anna Bullen*, teach me all thy Courage;
Thy Innocence, that makes the Heav'ns amaz'd:

And..

And the more guilty Angels blufh to fee.
Help me to pafs this *Rubicon* of Parting,
This mid-way Gulph that hangs 'twixt Earth and Sky !
Then that bleft Region, all beyond is mine,
And *Cæfar* was not half fo great as I.

Queen. Go ! be a lucky Harbinger for me ;
Tell all the Saints, and Cherubins, and Martyrs,
Tell all the Wrong'd, that now are righted there,
Till it fhall reach the high, *Imperial* Ear,
That *Anna Bullen* is a coming ftreight.

Roch. Wilt not embrace thy dying Brother firft ?
One Father and one Mother gave us Birth ;
And one Chaft, Innocent Natures Bed inclos'd us————
Thefe are our Parents Arms, and fo are thine.
Then all you Saints above, and Men below,
Bear Witnefs, and I vow it on my Death,
It is the greateft, firft, and only favour
I e're receiv'd from *Anna Bullen's* Perfon.

Queen. In fpite of Scandal, Malice, and the World ;
Nay, were the King and our vile Judges by,
Since Heav'n is fatisfy'd it is no Sin ;
I will embrace thee, think I've in my Arms,
Both Father, Mother, Sifter, Brother, all ;
And Envy cannot blame me now for this.

Roch. Thus, let thy Soul into my Bofom fly ;
That I may feel the ftroke of Death for thee ;
And when the fatal Ax hangs o're thy Head,
O may it lull Thee, and not ftrike thee dead ;
Softer than Infants Dreams, or with lefs pain,
Than 'tis to fleep, or to be born again———   [*Ex.* Roch. *to Ex-*

Queen. So, this is paft and vanquifht ! but behold   *ecution.*
A greater yet———Now I begin to dread———

Enter Diana, *with the young Princefs, and Women.*

Ah kind *Diana,* wonderful and good !
The pity that thou fhew'ft thy dying Friend,
This little one, I hope, will live to pay.

Dian. Ah Royal Miftrefs ! *England's* falling Star !
Beft Pattern that e're Earth receiv'd from Heav'n———

I

I need not fear thefe Eyes fhould fee you dye.
For e're that time, juft grief fhall ftrike me dead;
Or Torrents of thefe Tears will make me blind.

Queen. Come, lift her to my Arms, and let me kifs her,
For 'tis the laft kind Office you will do me.
Now let me prefs thy little Coral-Lips
With my dead pale ones now! and oh let me
Infufe fome of thy Mothers lateft Breath,
In Bleffings on thy tender, blooming Soul———
What's this that tempts me with a Mothers Fondnefs!
To break my Refolution, and upbraids me,
That I muft leave thee to a Father's Rage,
And yet more cruel Enemies to both?
Leave thee a Lamb, 'mongft Wolves; for all who've been
Thy Mothers Foes will certainly be thine.

Dian. Tygers, nor Devils! or what's more inhumane;
Envy of Mankind cannot be fo Curft.

Queen. See, fee *Diana*! by my Wrongs it weeps,
Weeps like a thing of Senfe, and not a Child;
Like one well underftood in Grief; the Tears
Drop fenfibly in order down its Cheeks;
And drowns its pretty Speech in thoughtful Sorrow.
Nothing could fhoot Infection through my Breaft,
But this; and this has done it———
Why weeps my Child? Ah, what a Queftion's that!

Dian. Behold! how't ftrives; and betwixt Tears and Throbs,
If it could form a Language, it would fpeak.

Queen. Strive not for Words, my Child; thefe little drops
Are far more Eloquent than Speech can be———
Be pitiful, my Lord; and thou, my kind
Diana, ever faithful to thy Queen;
When I am dead, as fhortly I fhall be,
Take this poor Babe, and carry't to the King;
Its Lips juft pregnant with its Mother's Fondnefs,
Perhaps he'l take her then into his Arms;
And tho' the favour were to me deny'd;
Steal there a Kifs of mine.
Say, 'tis the laft Requeft of *Anna Bullen*———

North. Remove the little Princefs
To her Apartment, where we ftreight will come.

L

And

And wait on her, as is the Queen's Command.

Queen.   Yet let me hold her but a moment longer,
And with this Kifs, that now muft be my laft,
Unlock a Secret, which Heav'n dictates to me.
If e're there is a Light that does tranfcend
Dark, humane Knowledge in the Breaft of Man,
Fate to forefee, there is a Light at Death,
And that now bids me fpeak.   Thou, little Child,
Shalt live to fee thy Mother's Wrongs o're paid
In many Bleffings on thy Womans State.
From this dark Calumny, in which I fet,
As in a Cloud; thou, like a Star, fhalt rife,
And awe the Southern World: That holy Tyrant,
Who binds all *Europe* with the Yoak of Confcience,
Holding his Feet upon the Necks of Kings;
Thou fhalt deftroy, and quite unloofe his Bonds,
And lay the Monfter trembling at thy Feet.
When this fhall come to pafs, the World fhall fee
Thy Mothers Innocence reviv'd in thee.

[*Ex. Women with the Princefs* Eliz.

North. Madam! with greater pain to me than Racks,
I'm forc'd to let you know your Brother's dead:
And that, alas! you muft prepare.

Queen. My Lord!
I thank you, you miftake your noble Office;
It is the Voice of Angels to wrong'd Martyrs;
The found of Cherubs trumpetting from Heav'n———
I've heard it faid, amongft our many Ends,
Beheading is the mildeft Death of any.
If it be fo; I thank my Gracious Lord:
For I was never us'd to pain——How fay you?

North. We cannot wifh you lefs, fince y'are to dye.
And if the Heads-man do as he's commanded,
'Twill be no more, than 'tis to drop afleep.

Queen. My Lord, I've but a little Neck;
Therefore I hope he'l not repeat his Blow;
But do it, like an Artift, at one ftroke.

North. There is no fear. He has particular Order.

Queen. Then let me go; Heav'n chides my fond delay———
But tell the King, I fay it as I juft

Am

Am going to dye; I both forgive, and bleſs him,
And thank him as my kindeſt Benefactor——
Firſt from an humble Maid he lifted me
To Honour ; then he took me to his Bed,
The higheſt State that I could be on Earth ;
And now, as if he thought he ne're could do
Enough for me, has mounted me to Heav'n——
   North. Mr. Lieutenant on, and lead the way.
   Queen. If 'tis no Sin to skip one moment now
Of what belongs to Heav'n ; let me remember
Poor *Piercy* once——Here, take this Innocent Kiſs,
A Token to you both———'Tis thine and his——
Farewel *! Diana.* Farewell to you all.
   Dian. A long farewell to all our Sexes Glory.
   Queen. Weep not for me ; but hear my dying Sentence.
Any that ſhall hereafter fall like me.
Falſly accus'd by wicked Men and Traytors ;
Tho' in this World y'are great, in Virtue ſtrong ;
Never Blaſpheme, and ſay that Heav'n does wrong ;
Nor think an undeſerved Death is hard ;
For Innocence is ſtill its own Reward.
And when th' Almighty makes a Saint, ſometimes
He acts by Contraries, and Villains Crimes,
Whilſt thus, their Malice always cheated is,
And leads us but the neareſt way to Bliſs.
   [*Exit Queen to Execution, with* Northumberland *and Guards.*

Enter Piercy *alone.*

   Pier. I dread the horrid deed is done, or now
A doing, elſe what means this ſudden Gloom
Clad o're the Morning Sky, and all Mankind :
All paſs with Horror by, with frighted Looks and Voice
Lift up to Heav'n, who ſees and hears in vain ;
Then ſhake their melancholly heads like Time :
A general Conſternation ſeizes all,
As if the Univerſal Empreſs of the World,
Nature it ſelf, were fled with *Anna Bullen*——

              Enter

Enter a Gentleman with a Hanckerchief ſtain'd with the Queens Blood.

Haſt thou beheld this great Eclipſe of Virtue?
Speak, is the Queen Beheaded? Haſt thou done
As I commanded?

   Gent. Sir, when the fatal blow I ſaw perform'd,
Swift as a Whirlewind, through the Crowd I ruſh't,
And, as the Blood from their rich Veſſels drain'd,
This Linnen with the Sacred Crimſon ſtain'd.

   Pier. Giv't me! and leave me to my ſelf a moment.
Now Sacred Drops, now Heavenly Nectar, firſt
I'le kiſs, then pledge you with a Dying Thirſt————
What's this! I feel my Soul beat at my Wound,
And bid me to remember now's the time;
Now to let out Life's Navigable Stream,
And mix it with this moſt Celeſtial Flood,
Thus, as kind Rivers to their Ocean run.
Firſt I'le deſcend by juſt degrees to Earth,
Thus on my Knees, and wing my Soul to Heaven,   [*Kneels.*
Where *Anna Bullen* waits her *Piercy's* coming;
And with this Bloody Sign the Pow'rs implore,
Like a poor Wretch, Ship-wrackt on ſome Lone-ſhoar,
Who ſpies a Sail far off, waves 'em his Hand
To come, and waft him from the Barren Land.

Enter Diana.

Behold the good *Diana*————By thoſe Tears,
Something of horror 'tis thou haſt to ſay.

   Dian. Alas! my Lord, what have you done?
Your Wound does bleed afreſh!
Your Looks are alter'd! all thoſe Maſculine Beauties,
That ſhone in your Illuſtrious Face, and made
The nobleſt brave Epitomy of Mankind,
Are vaniſht on a ſudden, and you hang
Like a pale Carcaſs on my trembling Arms————
Hah! let me run and call for help————I'le fetch
Your Father, fetch the King. Quick, let me go————

   Pier. O Bear me to ſome horrid Deſart rather,

Where

Where naught but Tygers, Wolves, and Panthers breed,
They are more merciful than King or Parent.
I feel, like the wrong'd *Patriarch*, a defire
To do fome fatal Mifchief with my End.
Stand by me; and Correct me with thy Virtue,
Elfe I fhall lofe the Duty of a Son,
And Subject; do a rafhnefs to be fam'd for,
Pull down a Show'r of Curfes on the Heads
Of this *Philiftim*-King, and Cruel Father.

 Dian. Still, ftill your looks grow Paler, and your ftrength
Decays! Oh let me call fome help. Who's there?

 Pier. Grief, like a fubtile Limbeck, by degrees,
With ftill Diffufion quite diffolves my heart,
And fteals by drops my Blood and Spirits away.
But firft *Diana*, I'le be juft to thee———
I doubt if I have ftrength to rife again———
       [*She raifes him upon his Knees.*
My Father made me Vow to be your Husband;
If I here die———I kneel that you'd forgive me;
But if I live, I'le keep my Promife to you.

 Dian. You Faint, you Sink, you Die; fome Creature help—

 Pier. Go, ftrive to Lave the Water of the Sea,
And Quench the burning *Ætna*, 'tis in vain,
And fo are *Efculapius* Remedies to me———
Look, fee'ft thou this, as long as I have this,
       [*Shews the Handkerchief.*
This here, to waft me o're Deaths dreadful Main,
I need no Sword, no Poifon, nor no Pain.

 Dian. What's that I fee? Your Blood? Your vital Blood!

 Pier. Yes! Of a Heart far Dearer than my own.
Now, now my Blood, my Crowd of Spirits, all
Rufh to behold, and with their Standard fall.

 Dian. Why ftand I here, like Marble made of Woe,
And run not for the Cure of both our Lives?
For fhou'd I ftay, I fhall betray my Love
In dying with him.   [*Exit* Diana *Running.*

 Pier. Thus when the Generous Lyon fees the Blood
Of his once Royal Mafter fhed like this;
Taking the Lawn, ftain'd with Imperial Gore,
At firft he Frowns, and then begins to Roar.

             Lafhes

Lashes his Sides; his Fiery Eye-balls rolls,
and with his awful Voice Revenge he calls;
Till finding no Relief, at length He's mute,
And Weeps, Tears falling from the Kingly Bruite;
Then gently on it, as his Death-bed lies,
And with a Groan, breaks his stout Heart, and Dies.   [*Dies.*

Enter Northumberland, *and* Gentlemen.

Gentl. He's dead! Alas, He's dead! W'are come too late!
North. Here let me fix till my Gray-Hairs shall rot,
Or turn to Snakes, to Plague this Aged Head;
And never more be lookt on to upbraid me!
This is a Punishment for what my Eyes
Unpitying saw; and now I feel, dear *Piercy,*
Thy Father's Curses on his own Head turn,
And thou art blest, and I alas, forlorn.

Enter King, Lords, Attendants, *and* Guards.

King. Whom mourn'st thou over? Whose dead Body's that?
North. 'Tis *Piercy*'s: You and all good Men shou'd weep,
For you have lost a faithful Queen, and I a Son.
King. Thy Tongue's too bold! Are all the Traitors dead?
North. *Norris,* and *Rochford,* and th'unhappy Queen,
Were all Beheaded in one Fatal Hour;
Yet all the Traitors are not dead.
King. What mean'st thou?
Say! Who has scap'd?
North. The Haughty *Blunt,* deckt with
Her proudest Ornaments of Gold and Jewels,
Came to behold their Ends upon the Scaffold,
And saw 'em with a Hellish Cruelty;
Till A*nna Bullen*'s Head lopp'd from her Body;
The brightest Ornament of that Person fell
Upon that wretched Womans Knees, as She
Was fitting to behold the Dismal sight:
The Trunkless Head with darting Eyes beheld her,
Making a motion with its Lips to speak,
As if they meant t'upbraid her Cursed Treason.

When

When ftreight the dreadful Accident fo ftruck her,
Swift as a Hind fhe gave a leap, and with
A fudden fhriek, fhe ftarted into Madnefs,
So fierce, that juft and fpeedy Death muft follow ;
Then uttering ftrange, and horrid Guilty Speeches,
In her diftraction fhe accus'd her felf,
And *Woolfey :* Talkt the Queen was Innocent ;
Saying, the Letters found within her Clofet
Were falfe, and plac'd by them to ruine Her :
For which her Cruel Ghoft, fhe faid, did haunt her.

    King. Where is the Traitor *Woolfey* ?
    North. Fled to *Efher.*
    King. Go you in Perfon, and fecure the Villain
Many foul Caufes claim his forfeit Life ;
But if I find him Guilty in the leaft,
Of a Contrivance with this Curfed Woman ;
(Though the Queen juftly merited her End)
I'le Rack his Soul out with a thoufand Tortures.

    North. 'Twill be fome joy to my Revenge and *Piercy's.*
    King. For thy Sons Death, thy King fhall be a Mourner—
Now Heav'n vouchfafe to Pardon till this time,
What I by Sycophants Advice have done,
I will be Abfolute, and Reign alone :
For where's a Statefman fam'd for juft and wife ;
But makes our Failings, ftill, his aim to Rife ?
If Subjects thus their Monarchs Wills reftrain ;
'Tis they are Kings ; for them we idly Reign :
Then I'le firft break the Yoak ; this Maxim ftill
fhall be my Guide (*A Prince can do no Ill* !)
In fpite of Slaves, his Genius let him truft ;
For Heav'n n'ere made a King, but made him juft.

                        [*Exeunt omnes.*

E P I-

EPILOGUE.

WEll, Sirs! Your kind Opinion now, I pray,
    Of this our neither Whig nor Tory-Play;
    To blow such Coales our Conscious Muse denies;
Wit, Sacred Wit, such Subjects should despise.
The Author saies his Heliconian stream,
Is not yet drain'd to such a low extream.
To abuse one Party with a Cursed Play,
And Bribe the other for a large third Day.
Like Gladiators then, you streight resort;
And Crowd to make your Nero-Faction sport.
But what's more strange, that Men of sense shou'd do it!
For Worrying one another, Pay the Poet:
So Butchers at a Baiting, take delight,
For him that keeps the Bears, to Roar and Fight;
Both Friends and Foes, such Authors make their Game,
Who have your Money, that was all their Ayme:
No matter for the Play, nor for their Wit;
The better Farce is Acted in the Pit.
Both Parties to be cheated, well agree;
And swallow any Nonsense, so it be
With Faction fac'd, and guilt with Loyalty.
Here's such a Rout with Whigging and with Torying,
That you neglect your dear-lov'd sin of Whoring:
The Visor-mask, that ventur'd her Half-Crown,
Finding no hopes but here to be undone;
Like a Cast Mistress, past her dear-delight,
Turns Godly streight, and goes to Church in spite;
And does not doubt, since you are grown so fickle,
To find more Cullies in a Conventicle.
We on the Stage stand still, and are content,
To see you Act what we should Represent.
You use us like the Women that you Woe;
You make us sport, and Pay us for it too.
Well, w' are resolv'd that in our next Play-Bill,
To Print at large a Tryal of your skill;
And that five hundred Monsters are to fight,
Then more will run to see so strange a sight,
Than the Morocco, or the Muscovite.

FINIS.